Kim Young-sam
and the
New Korea

Bonus Books, Inc., Chicago

96 95 94 93 92   5 4 3 2 1

Library of Congress Catalog Card Number: 92-74148

International Standard Book Number: 0-929387-89-9

Bonus Books, Inc.
160 East Illinois Street
Chicago, Illinois 60611

Printed in the United States of America

Composition by Point West, Inc., Carol Stream, IL

Contents

one

The miracle on the Han

Kim Young-sam, a Korean politician now in his mid-sixties, says he can hardly believe his eyes when he looks around him in the capital city of Seoul or even at his own home island in the southeast of the country. "For those of us who knew Korea in the late 1950s, the spectacle of contemporary Seoul and Korea in 1992 is sometimes a shock," he says. Like many foreign visitors, he finds it hard to connect the modern metropolis of 10.5 million people—frenetic with traffic, goods, and people—with those early post-Korean War years when destruction and poverty haunted the whole country.

Seoul today is a city of tree-lined avenues. Its people reside in neat little villas and huge public housing units. They shop at big, flashy department stores as well as at thousands of small, well-kept artisan shops. Huge metal-working factories and hermetically sealed electronics plants create the industrial pulse in suburbia. One is dazzled by the trendy, high-fashion appearance of the city's young people. The new, international hotels—with their Western flavor—would be unthinkable in the old, traditional Korea.

At first glance, the visitor finds no trace of those years of horror during and after the Korean War only 40 years earlier. That may be one reason why the Korean War remains "the forgotten war" in the U.S., despite heavy American casualties. Even in Korea itself, the conflict is largely ignored if not forgotten by a new generation of Koreans.

Today South Korea is a modern nation, rapidly reaching economic levels that would soon put it among the major industrialized countries. The statistics make that abundantly clear: Korea, a small country about the size of Indiana, has few natural resources in the South. Arable land is sparse, and less than 11 percent can be farmed. Korea now has 43 million people; and its rapid, earlier population growth is now slowing to the same rates as in the industrialized West. Past growth had been so swift that today's Korea has the highest population density per square mile of arable land in the whole world.

However, by the end of 1991, per capita gross national product had reached $6,498. (U.S. per capita gross national product in 1991 was $22,550.) And, Korea's exports had risen to $71.9 billion, making Korea the fourteenth largest exporter in the world. (In 1987, in comparison, the country's per capita gross national product was $3,110 and exports stood at $47.9 billion.) As Kim Young-sam points out, one of the ironies of the present situation is that South Korea soon may be facing a shortage of skilled labor as its population levels off.

In a sense, the Koreans took the traditional way to wealth: between 1961 and 1986, industrial modernization had replaced agriculture as the economic mainstay of Korea. Agriculture and fisheries, which had accounted for 37 percent of total production in 1960, fell to only 8 percent in 1991. Manufacturing has doubled as a percentage of the gross national product, from 14 percent to 28 percent. Furthermore, the Koreans changed the nature of what they produced—chemicals, electronics, machinery, automobiles, and petrochemicals now dominated an increasingly sophisticated industrial base. Automobile production, that bellwether of modern industry, has jumped phenomenally with Korea ranked as the world's tenth largest manufacturer of motor vehicles in 1991.

Kim asserts, "Now we live in an industrial society, and while some of my countrymen don't seem to realize it, we have a whole new set of problems, leaving in the past those problems of an agrarian society that we argued over for so long." Said differently, Korea has made social and economic gains that are hard to convey in abstract economic growth figures. In data from 1991, these gains lend weight to Kim's general argument that the rapid industrial expansion had produced The New Korea:

Life expectancy had increased to 68.2 years for males and 75.9 years for females (and now stands at about the level of the most developed countries).

Virtually all Koreans were now covered by medical health insurance.

Spending on cultural, educational and recreational activities in the average urban household had increased markedly.

Over the last 32 years, food prices had dropped in relative terms for the average householder by 42 percent.

While the housing demand still outpaced supply, a program to build two million new units had been launched by the government and was making considerable progress.

More than 50 percent of all Korean college-aged males and more than 24 percent of Korean females were attending university. (In Korea's young population, one out of every two Korean males is college educated and one out of every four females attends college.)

Nearly all Korean households had such modern appliances as telephones, automatic rice cookers, television sets, washing machines, and refrigerators.

It has become fashionable to refer to the success of the Korean economy as "the miracle on the Han", the Han being the broad river that flows through the capital of Seoul. The term suggests a replay of "the miracle on the Rhine" so often used to refer to the rebuilding of West Germany after World War II. But, in its most literal sense, the analogy is a mistake. Kim Young-sam points out, "As great as the German success was, you have to remember that the German Federal Republic *rebuilt* a role for German industry and technology." Kim reminds non-Koreans that the Germans already had a base of trained industrial and technological workers. This workforce had established Germany as a leading industrial nation in the world long before the Nazi regime brought on the World War II catastrophe. "But in Korea, we came out of an almost feudal, agrarian society—victims of the Japanese occupation of 50 years. Whatever Tokyo did here by way of modernization was only to prop up the Japanese economy itself. Since liberation, we actually turned Korea into a modern entrepreneurial society in less than half a century."

There are few examples of anything else like it in history; even the other "dragons"—the other prospering East Asian states of Taiwan, Hong Kong, Singapore—all have had special advantages in the prewar and postwar eras that Korea did not. Perhaps even more incredible, "the Miracle on the Han" has taken place during a period of great domestic political instability. While the economy was moving ahead rapidly, an authoritarian government ruled. That government suppressed a democratic opposition, one of whose most prominent leaders during this whole 30-year period was Kim Young-sam.

Kim compares his political career to mountain climbing. In fact, in the 1960s, he had created a mountain-climbing club. No simple recreational organization, that club was and is still one of the most important and sophisticated political groupings in the country. It has been a long and precarious climb for Kim. But he now sees himself within sight of the highest peak. And he has an almost messianic belief that he can give Korea the kind of stable, democratic rule that history and the internal play of political ambitions has not permitted the country through most of the period since its liberation in 1945.

Kim's program has three goals, and he says none can be achieved without the realization of the other two:

1. Build a "mature" political democracy in Korea.

2. Continue economic prosperity through a wise development program.

3. Through patience and quiet resolve, bring about the reunification of the country split between two warring halves since 1945.

Kim says that "by building on the remarkable economic achievements of the past 30 years, Korea can now move up to a new plateau of freedom with stability and prosperity. He sees his role as a mediator, as a compromiser, as someone who builds a synthesis of others' ideas and ambitions. Putting together the right political combination to get a job done in government (or outside it) is what Kim thinks is his chief talent. Most political observers in Korea agree. And, it's an invaluable asset in overcoming the history of broken promises and fratricidal conflict inside the Republic of Korea.

Kim frankly acknowledges the bitterness and regional, sectarian history of post-World War II politics. He argues that he has always tried to respect the dignity and sincerity of his opponents. He recalls that after former President Park Chung-hee, his old and bitter enemy, was brutally assassinated in 1979—and against the advice of his political allies—he demonstrated his reconciliation by attending the funeral at the gravesite. Kim reflects, "He was our president and deserved that kind of respect even though I had always disagreed with him and had been badly treated by him. I was, in fact, one of his victims."

President Roh Tae-woo's Declaration of Democratic Reforms on June 29, 1987, was a milestone in the development of a plural, democratic state in the Republic of Korea. It might have been just another empty gesture had Kim not acted to merge his parliamentary opposition with the ruling party. Now it has Kim's imprimatur. It has permitted the kind of cooperation between the executive and the legislative branches that has been rare in the Republic of Korea's history. Kim would argue, furthermore, that had he not made his pact with Roh, the country would again be facing the kind of fractured presidential campaign which resulted in Roh's election, with only a 34 percent plurality of the popular vote. It was this kind of short-circuiting of the democratic process that had put the legitimacy of the regime in question since the military came to power in 1960. Kim says that his role now "is to bind up the wounds of my country, to use our successful economic program as the underpinning for another giant step forward toward full democracy." Kim is the only leader on the current political scene with the skill and credentials to succeed in achieving this goal. He is a leader—who for more than two decades was the head of the democratic opposition to a highly centralized, oppressive regime, and who is seen by many of his fellow Koreans as a long-time martyr to democratic ideals.

Certainly, the economic leap that Korea has taken is a paramount consideration—not only in Kim's plans for his country but on how the Koreans regard themselves. Korea's growth over the past 30 years has been spectacular in absolute terms. It is all the more sensational since the country advanced in two generations from being one of the poorest nations in the world to the very threshold of joining today's industrialized elite. The Republic of Korea's economy now is the thirteenth largest in the world. And all this has been achieved despite high population density and growth, lack of natural resources, and a need to maintain one of the world's largest military establishments.

In 1962, when the Republic of Korea launched its first five-year development plan, its per capita income was only $81. Growing at no less than 80-fold, at an average rate of 16.3 percent, gross national product per capita climbed by 1991 to the $6,498 figure. With an annual growth rate of 8.6 percent, real gross national product grew nearly 12-fold. Of course, no single factor can account for this staggering rate of progress—certainly nothing to be found on the computer printouts of the "scientists" in the economics fraternity. Observers have cited an array of elements in the Korean environment to explain the phenomenon.

One factor has certainly been an outward-looking, export-oriented strategy for economic development, which has enabled Korea to exploit its comparative advantages in the international marketplace. It permitted the Koreans to use economies of scale to their full advantage. Korean industry has also adroitly incorporated foreign technologies into its own inventory of skills. As a result, from 1961 to 1991, Korean exports grew at an average rate of 29.7 percent per year. There is little argument among most observers that throughout this period the rapid growth of exports was a primary engine of overall economic growth.

Kim would argue that one of the most important factors in the economic miracle—one that few economists are willing to concede—"is the very nature of our people. Unless you have an understanding of the Korean mentality, you cannot appreciate why we were able to accomplish so much in spite of all the obstacles, some of which, ironically, we ourselves may have put in our own way."

One of those fundamental Korean characteristics is a fanatical dedication to education. There is no doubt that the economic miracle can, to some extent, be ascribed to a high level of educational achievement, particularly when set against the lack of a drive for better education in some other underdeveloped countries. The penchant for education has come to a large extent from a traditional source: The Confucian ethic with its emphasis on education and formal examination.

By the early 1960s, the Koreans had achieved 80 percent literacy, an unheard of level for a Third World country. With increasing incomes, the drive for education intensified. Enrollment in colleges and universities advanced from 140,000 in 1966 to 1,127,077 by 1990. As a result, 8.9 percent of the population has at a minimum attended college. Without this increase in educational levels, it would not have been possible for the Korean workforce to enter more sophisticated industries as economic growth continued.

It is also clearly true that a favorable international environment aided the Republic of Korea's expansion during this period. One element was, of course, the massive inflow of American aid. When U.S. direct aid to the Korean economy ended in the mid-1970s, the Republic of Korea had received a total of $15.86 billion in grants and loans for civilian and military purposes. This included $8.79 billion for economic aid and $7.07 billion for military aid. (The reader is reminded of two important qualifications to these figures, however: Most of this capital was in 1950s-1960s dollars so the actual worth of the aid is understated. And although the portion characterized as military aid largely covered weapons and other war-making materials, much of the military aid, too, helped build the economy as well. It paid, for example, for the rental of military-base land and the procurement of local products. Nor does the military figure include the wages of the American soldiers posted in South Korea or their private spending in the economy.)

There is little doubt that South Korean industry came

of age in a benign period in the world economy, as well. The long post-World War II peace, despite its grim threat of a possible nuclear holocaust, has been a prosperous time. Until the late 1970s, the provisions of the General Agreement on Tariffs and Trade (GATT) and its discipline were intact, and markets in the U.S. and other countries were open to Korean exports. Furthermore, world trade was expanding at a rapid clip—14.9 percent in real terms from 1962 to 1979. Flourishing Korean exports benefited from the high rates of growth in the Organization for Economic Cooperation and Development (OECD) countries, particularly in the United States.

One observer, Alice H. Amsden,[1] has argued that the Koreans are a paradigm of what she has labeled "late industrialization".

This evolutionary stage is based on "learning" rather than what she calls "development" and "innovation", phases which she ascribes to the earlier industrialization processes in Britain, Germany, and the United States, and to Japan, respectively. Ms. Amsden argues that it was the interventionist measures of the Korean regime that were the principal propellant in Korean development. Such an approach is, of course, at odds with the views of those proponents of market forces as the best stimulant of economic development. Amsden's rather intense polemic is obviously aimed at answering and disputing the market-forces advocates who are so fashionable today. But, there are also obvious disasters that befell interventionist strategies and policies among a great number, if not most, of the other underdeveloped countries during this same period.

At independence in 1948, for example, India had inherited not only the largest industrial sector among underdeveloped nations but a significant entrepreneurial community and the best-trained planners in the Third World. To all this was added access to large sterling balances and to enormous borrowed resources and grant aid. Yet the whole interventionist process was such a failure that future generations of Indians will be paying for it.

Again, we should return to the simple argument of Kim Young-sam that there is a special quality about Korean society. Could such peculiarities account for the Korean achievement and for Korea taking such a different course than most other underdeveloped countries?

Kim's explanation helps one to understand the enormous difficulties which faced government planners immediately following the Korean War. The regime had to cope with three grim realities:

> The country was poor in natural resources—the mineral wealth of the peninsula was located in the North. The South had only a small supply of poor quality anthracite coal.

> The North was also home to most major industrial undertakings, their roots dating back to the era of the Japanese Occupation.

> The country was hard put to feed itself. True, in early Japanese times, Korea had been an exporter of agricultural produce, mostly rice to Japan. But in the late 1930s and during the 1940s, the demands on the Japanese empire grew because of the war on the Chinese mainland which later extended to Southeast Asia and the Pacific. Korea was hard put to feed itself. As a result, exports dwindled and food consumption declined inside the country. "I am old enough to remember when just having enough to fill their stomachs was a problem for most of my people," Kim Young-sam recalls, speaking of his childhood after World War II.

Because of these factors, the planners of a newly independent Korea had to think in terms of importing raw materials as well as necessary consumer goods in the early period. The burgeoning population also made unemployment a major concern of the government. And there were the demands of the unresolved conflict with North Korea—stayed only by an armistice. A German-style evolution toward two internationally recognized regimes on both sides of the Iron Curtain never took place, at least not until the collapse of the Soviet Union in 1989. That meant that in addition to military aid from the U.S., the post-Korean War regimes have had to maintain significant and expensive military forces.

"Although it may sound strange or contradictory, the fear that stemmed from the constant Communist threat may have actually helped us," Kim says. "It galvanized our will, because we knew what would happen if we fell behind the North." As Kim argues, the contest with North Korea was a spur to the rapid economic growth of the Republic of Korea. In the 1950s, it was generally believed that the North was making more rapid economic progress than the South because of the North's relatively massive investment in heavy industrial plant expansion, for military purposes and in pursuit of the Soviet model.

In the 1950s, growth in the South was indeed unimpressive. Korea was largely a traditional, closed, agrarian economy, with two-thirds of the population living on the land. The economy in this period coupled a vicious circle of poverty with the compounding problems of political instability, rampant inflation, and an inability to meet the most basic needs of consumers. What little industrial development which had existed in the South was destroyed in the Korean War. Economic policy-making fluctuated, beset by a lack of planning experience on the Korean side and conflicting views about the appropriate strategies for Korea within the U.S. Agency for International Development (AID) mission. The rapid growth of population, accelerating urbanization, and consequent unemployment exacerbated all the other problems.

The Republic of Korea's first government under President Syngman Rhee was largely occupied with postwar reconstruction. Maintenance of public order also became a major governmental challenge because of growing resentment and agitation against this regime. However, the Rhee government succeeded in setting the stage for an important development through a program of land reform. The land tenure settlement brought about a significantly more level distribution of income among the 66 percent of the population which remained on the land into the 1960s. And the Korean War, with all its destruction, further leveled the incomes of the population in the South. The net result: The annual average rate of growth of the gross national product during the nine-year period following the War, 1953-62, was only 3.7 percent; and that of the per capita gross national product was a meager 0.7 percent.

When Korea launched its drive for economic development in 1961, it had to decide the crucial issue of how to allocate its severely limited finances among the different economic sectors. A decision was made to push for the development of light industry, ignoring agriculture for the time being, since agricultural development requires disproportionately large capital outlays in its early stages. Further, those expenditures need plenty of time to realize a significant return.

Into the 1960s, the orthodoxy of import substitution reigned. Local manufacturers were subsidized by making capital available for them to create marketable goods. At the same time, the competing imports to these goods were kept out by tariffs and non-tariff barriers. Because the manufacturers were chiefly supplying domestic needs, Korean industry grew little. And most of this growth was confined to light industry.

After Maj. Gen. Park Chung-hee's military coup in 1961, a radical change in economic policy and strategy took place. Park, the son of impoverished peasant farmers, had attended Japanese military academies and served in the Japanese army. With this background and the ample evidence that Japan was moving ahead rapidly in reasserting its pre-War position as a major factor in world trade, it was only natural that Park was to look to the Japanese model.

Relations between Japan, the former colonial power, and Korea, the former colony, have been sensitive and sometimes embittered. Despite this, the Koreans have used Japan as an economic development model for some parts of their economy. Japan has also been an important trading partner for Korea and, most of all, a source of managerial as well as technical expertise.

The Park regime set out almost immediately to normalize South Korea's relations with Japan. It then abandoned the attempt to create protected markets inside the country. Following the Japanese lead, Korea achieved a major success in the 1960s by pointing the economy in the direction of exports. The country made quick gains in the international markets, particularly in textiles. The regime also adopted economic planning, but it was not a Soviet-style command economy with a huge government sector like that which India and some other Third World nations attempted to create in the 1950s. Korea's approach was more in the Western style of target planning.

Still the Koreans were adventurous, often against

outside advice and in the face of the worst experiences of other countries. For example, Korea made an important commitment to the steel industry. To the chagrin of some of the U.S. American International Development (AID) advisers and skeptical Japanese (who nevertheless were willing to sell and finance the equipment), the government went ahead with a fullscale steelworks. Perhaps it goes without saying that steel has been one of the great Korean success stories.

The first two five-year economic development schemes—covering the 1962-66 and 1967-71 periods—aimed at increasing investment in manufacturing and exports. The manufacturing sector grew at an average rate of 15 percent in the first five years and 21.1 percent in the second five years. Total investment averaged 20 percent of gross national product during the first period and 30 percent of gross national product during the second five years. Even more importantly, domestic savings expanded rapidly enough to account for half the investment during the second period as commodity exports grew at the rate of 44 percent during the first period and 35 percent during the second.

There were many mistakes: One of the first moves of the new military regime was to put the central bank under the control of the government. Certainly, this permitted rapid implementation of government policies. It also allowed government participation through equity holdings in the commercial banks. But, it was also linked to the continuing problem of inflation. Government interference in the price structure often led to the bankruptcy of otherwise able firms. Some of the firms favored by the government developed into today's *chaebol*, the huge conglomerates that today dominate the Korean economy and which are also now being charged in some quarters with blocking the initiative of smaller companies. Additionally, income distribution became increasingly skewed. Finally, although the Korean population itself was pursuing education at all costs, it can be argued that the government did not support education enough.

Yet having said all that, clear hindsight reveals that the Korean government's planners persevered and stumbled on and—to a large extent—got it right. Recognizing South Korea's meager natural resources and the modest domestic market, the new economic policy of the "first period" set out to emphasize exports and maximize Korea's comparative advantage in international markets. The government provided export subsidies and incentives including various tax exemptions. It also reduced rates for public utilities, provided tariff rebates for imported products destined for re-export, simplified customs procedures, and accelerated depreciation allowances. Ironically, these measures of government intervention permitted Korean exporters to operate as though they were part of a free-trade economy. This even included a shift from a list of negative import restrictions to a set of positive inducements.

Korea needed enormous investment to break its vicious circle (of poverty, political instability, and increased poverty) and to compensate for the lack of domestic savings. Incentives to attract the enormous amount of needed foreign capital were made an important part of the program. Contrary to many other Third World governments at the time, Korea even undertook to guarantee foreign investment under its Foreign Capital Promotion Act of 1966. Drawn by the higher turnover rate, this capital moved mainly into light manufacturing including textiles. Thus foreign capital made up 50 percent of investment during the 1962-71 period.

The 1960s were also a time of great institutional change. Tax administration was revamped, an Export Promotion Council was formed, and the five-year plans were drafted under the supervision of an Economic Planning Board (EPB) founded in 1962. Functioning as a super-ministry, the EPB was the main actor in the government's program of outwardly oriented economic strategies. The deputy prime minister concurrently held the portfolio of minister of economic planning while acting as the main force in directing the economy. Unlike many other under-developed countries, the Korean EPB was both a planning and a management institution, directly participating in the administration of decisions on economic strategy. Furthermore, the deputy prime minister held a whip hand in directing the activities of other ministries because of the budget functions of the EPB.

Changing world economic conditions in the 1970s and the mistakes made in the 1960s led the Koreans to believe there was a need for a revised or new national strategy. Seoul was faced with a declining U.S. military presence in the Far East but no respite from the threat of the Communist North. So, it decided to build its own defense industry. There was also more than a hint of mounting protectionism in the U.S. and Japan to the growth of Korean exports, especially against textiles and the expanding garment trade. This led the Korean government to modify its outward-looking development program by returning to import substitution, particularly in heavy chemicals and in agriculture. Rising living standards and incomes were another motivation behind this decision: The Republic of Korea was losing its comparative cost advantage by using unskilled labor to manufacture such exports as plywood, footwear, and textiles. It was clear that the economy had to move to more sophisticated products.

The return to import substitution was initially a disaster. The chemical and heavy machinery industries were extremely capital intensive and needed long periods to mature. Overly optimistic world trade estimates and an inflationary financial system made many of the projects unwise.

Meanwhile, the government acknowledged the growing disparity of income between urban and rural areas and set out to widen and enlarge the agricultural sector. The *Saemaul Undong* (New Community Development Movement) was designed to encourage economic and social development in the villages through a self-help program aided by matching central government funds. The government also set up a new system of rice subsidies whereby a higher rice price would be paid producers while public funds would subsidize a lower selling price to consumers. Along with the simultaneous introduction of new seed varieties, additional irrigation, mechanization, and insecticides; the new system led to a dramatic rise in rice production. So successful was the program— although it exacted costs and created new social problems down the road—that yields exceeded those in Japan and reached one of the highest levels in the world.

Another important factor for the Republic of Korea was the export of construction services to the Middle East. These construction contracts helped to pay for the quadrupling of imported energy costs in 1973-74. They also helped to relieve the pressure on the balance of payments by remitting almost $15 billion by the end of 1978 from the Middle East alone. Korean companies and workers, of course, gained valuable experience from these contracts. But, there were negative effects, too: The export of skilled labor in such large quantities pushed up wages and thus widened the gap between skilled and unskilled workers, intensifying income distribution disparities. The inflow of foreign exchange aggravated inflation by forcing an increase in the money supply.

Nevertheless, high growth rates continued, but they were accompanied by some negative aspects, including continued high inflation and a rapid rise in real wages (particularly in the heavy industrial sector). The latter aggravated the problem of the disproportionate expansion of heavy industry. The rising labor costs adversely affected the price of Korean exports. Regional and income disparities generally worsened. And Korea learned that the price of success was a growing vulnerability to world market fluctuations.

In April 1979, following the dramatic political events of that year—including the assassination of the president—the government announced a stabilization program to restructure the economy. It set out to cut back on liquidity through banking reform and tighter restraint on money. The government temporarily suspended a good part of the investment in heavy industry and returned to encouraging the development of light industrial projects. And to force adjustments in the price structure, the government decontrolled prices on many items. Import liberalization was stepped up by reducing tariffs and beginning to wipe out non-tariff import barriers. Between 1979 and 1988, a large part of the non-tariff barriers on industrial products was removed. Tariffs were reduced from 25 percent to 17 percent. The government enacted the Anti-Monopoly Act in 1981 in an effort to reduce monopolistic practices and promote competition in all industries.

These moves were all seen as efforts to shift from government controls to market mechanisms. Despite the disruptions, prices remained stable, the balance of payments stayed healthy, and the high grow rates continued. Those trends persisted until 1988 when the internal and the external environments began to deteriorate. Kim says what is required now is a fresh approach to the new international economic situation.

two

Kim Young-sam, politician and statesman

As a high-school student, Kim wrote the symbols for "Future President of Korea: Kim Young-sam" in Chinese calligraphy and hung the statement in his study room. His friends ridiculed him for it. The adolescent's ambition seemed all the more absurd in a country just escaping a half century of bitter Japanese occupation. But Kim's youthful dream may soon become a reality.

Kim's forty-year career in Korean politics parallels the history of the trials and tribulations of his nation. Kim is knowledgeable about the traditions of Korea's isolated past as The Hermit Kingdom. He understands the important changes which took place in the nineteenth century. And he experienced first hand the twisted attempt at forced modernization under Japanese colonialism.

Kim's story begins on the little island of Gujae off the southeast coast of the Korean peninsula. He was born there in 1927, the only son in a family with five sisters. Unlike politicians the world over, Kim does not claim to have risen from a background of poverty and ignorance. He freely admits that his father was a wealthy fish-industry entrepreneur—dried anchovies—a business which his 82-year old father still owns and runs today.

Kim, who claims descent from the old Korean man-darinate, the *Yangban*, comes from a Christian (Presbyterian) family. His grandfather, himself a convert, built the first church on Gujae and helped bring the remaining islanders to Christianity. The child Kim early expressed an interest in the arts and has been a lifelong calligrapher, a writer of the intricate Chinese ideographs. These complicated symbols are an art form which is the essence of East Asian cultural history, as well as a means of communication that links the verbal languages of a dozen national cultures. Kim started at five to learn the use of the brush. The hobby has stood him in good stead. His family recalls how it provided an outlet for his frustration during the long years of imprisonment and house arrest as a political dissident.

But whatever the Kim family's material well-being, Kim could not escape the bitter history of his country over the last century. At seven, he was sent off to an elementary school located at some distance from his home. And now in his sixties, he still recalls his loneliness and how his political career has forced him into living most of his years "constantly on the road." The young Kim especially missed his mother, and he would walk home on Saturday night across a small mountain just to see her for a few hours before returning to the school. She passed away during the Korean War. In the Korean Confucian tradition, his remembrance of her as a gentle and admirable woman remains an important part of his spiritual life.

The school he attended was typical of the Japanese colonial period in Korea. Two-thirds of the students were from the emigrant Japanese families who had taken over Korean land or worked for the colonial government. They had special perquisites under the colonial regime. Although the Koreans who attended the school were considered privileged, Kim found life there miserable. Tokyo was bogged down in a war in China. Japanese militarism and nationalism were gaining the upper hand, and their impact was felt in Korea, too. Japanese policy dictated that every effort be made to wipe out the Korean language, its indigenous script, *Han'gul*, and the Korean identity.

The Japanese teachers were openly derisive and discriminatory toward the Korean youngsters, and Kim spent much of his time in fights with his Japanese classmates. Kim acknowledges today that his frays with the Japanese students had less to do with Korean nationalism and patriotism than the simple reaction to their arrogance and bullying. His Korean schoolmates remember him as smaller than many of his opponents, but he was a feisty little kid who managed to hold his own. A good wrestler and swimmer, he became the natural leader of the Korean students. The friction culminated in a gang fight between the Korean and Japanese students in his junior year which caused him to be expelled from the school. This happened at nearly the climactic moment of the Pacific War— with the defeat of the Japanese and the end of their occupation.

After the liberation, Kim went on to the famous

Kyong-nam Middle School, where for five years he was a well respected student. He left behind his fisticuffs of the earlier period. Although not a brilliant scholar, he maintained good grades and developed a keen interest in history, philosophy, and literature. He was a popular member of the soccer team, an experience which he contends taught him the importance of team work and the value of friendship.

In 1948, Kim entered Seoul National University, the premier Korean university, where he continued his interest in political science and philosophy. He was a gifted public speaker and, in his sophomore year, received the Ministry of Foreign Affairs Award in a speech contest. At that time he met then-foreign minister, Chang Taek-sang, a fervent anti-Communist and a very successful politician. He was to become Kim's mentor. Only two years later, while Kim was still a college junior, when Chang decided to run for elective office, he asked Kim to be his campaign director.

It was exactly the opportunity Kim had been looking for, and he reveled in his new role when Chang was successful and entered the National Assembly. He learned the techniques of professional politicians; and most importantly, he became an even better public speaker. All this was taking place on the eve of Korea's great postwar catastrophe, the Communist-sponsored North's invasion of the American-occupied South. For four long years, the bitter and bloody war raged up and down the peninsula. Kim enlisted in the army as an information specialist, and he broadcasted messages directed toward the Northern soldiers from a secret studio in the Korean ministry of defense. Early in the conflict, the superior Communist forces pushed the U.N. troops into the so-called Pusan Perimeter. It was a debacle for the Allies, and the fighting around that southeastern port cut Kim off from seeing his family.

After eight months, Kim was able to rejoin Chang as his assistant and to continue his university career on a part-time basis. He graduated in 1952. His father urged him to marry young; and a traditional, arranged union took place with Son Myung Soon, daughter of a manufacturer of traditional Korean rubber shoes in the city of Masan. Kim was less obedient about his choice of a career. Much to his father's chagrin, Kim decided to run for a seat in the National Assembly. It was unheard of for someone so young in Korea's age-honoring Confucian society to aspire to such an esteemed position. But Kim had much going for him: He was already well known in his home environs. He was the *only* college graduate on Gujae in a Korean society which puts education on the highest pedestal. He had been a secretary to Chang, who had moved into the prime ministry and then become vice speaker of the assembly. And he was an accomplished orator. None of this was enough, however, to persuade his father. He thought Kim would not be able to raise the necessary campaign funds because Kim was so young. Kim proved his father, who reluctantly went along with the idea in the end, and everyone else wrong. At 25 he was elected as the youngest member of the National Assembly ever—a record that still holds.

Kim was a young and enthusiastic—even bumptious—assemblyman. He did not hesitate to denounce the government for its increasingly autocratic methods. President Syngman Rhee, who had come back from exile in the U.S. to head the Korean government in the American-occupied South, didn't appreciate Kim's attacks. In a dramatic personal encounter, Kim met Rhee and told him that as the old and honored "father of the country," Rhee should retire and leave the field to younger people, assuming an elder statesman's role. The older man turned on his heel without a word and walked away.

Rejected by Rhee's ruling Liberal Party as a candidate, Kim moved to Pusan—South Korea's growing second city and principal port. However, he lost this campaign for the National Assembly. To this day, he believes that the loss was more due to ballot-box stuffing than to the popularity of the then Pusan mayor who was his opponent. But Kim was not about to give up his political activity; and, in 1959, he was one of the organizers of the campaign for the presidency of Jo Byung Ok. Whether Jo could have been successful is doubtful, given the methods of the Rhee regime; but, in any case, the elderly Jo died during the campaign and before the elections.

The abuses of the Rhee regime finally exploded in 1960, bringing what was to become known as the April 19th Students' Revolution to the streets of Seoul. The events saw Kim's house in Seoul turned into a command center for the youthful revolutionaries. After weeks of demonstrations—and unfortunate deaths and injuries to the students when the political police fired on them—the fall of the Rhee regime gave Kim a new opportunity. He was elected to the fifth National Assembly on the rolls of the Democratic Party and immediately became embroiled in a fight over party leadership. The older generation of party leadership, who had come up as anti-Japanese revolutionaries, was being challenged by a new generation of politicians, who had come forward after the liberation. It was characteristic of Kim that, although the younger group offered him the post of National Defense Minister, he chose to ally himself with the veteran anti-Communists and rejected the offer. This led to a split in the party; and Kim became the chief of a new party until it, too, broke up in 1961 in the fracturing of the political scene which followed the demise of Rhee's strongarm rule and the emergence of a military government.

Again, Kim turned this government crisis into an opportunity and organized a new caucus in the National Assembly. In the rapidly degenerating situation under President Chang Myun, the vice president in the Rhee regime, Kim took strong positions for a cleanup of the increasingly corrupt and chaotic Korean political scene. He advocated a greater adherence to democratic principles and the reunification of the country. Kim strongly endorsed a program of exchanges with the North. In this, he was supported by students and the Koreans of dispersed families of Northern origin who had fled the Communists. Kim took this stand even against opposition from fellow conservatives who feared that, in the troubled South Korean environment, the Pyongyang regime would use these gestures to undermine the South. Such is the strength of Kim's commitment to unification.

"Looking back now from the 1990s," Kim says, "that period may have been the most difficult for me. I understood that we were threatened from the North; I knew we had to clean up our own back yard; but I wanted it to be done by democratic civilian methods, not by the military, whose job it was to defend us from the outside." When the Korean army moved to seize power, even the American advisers did not know why. When the military filled the vacuum created by the breakdown of the Chang government, Kim was in his home district. By the time he got to Seoul, he found his fellow politicians scattering in all directions literally looking for a place to hide when a military coup occurred on May 16, 1981.

Kim was offered exile in the United States, but he refused. "I knew my place was here in Korea, with the rest of my fellow Koreans, to experience whatever would come," he says now. And he set about organizing a new democratic party with its aims of ending military government and setting up a civilian one. On May 22, 1963, he secretly organized a demonstration against the military administration with the help of students and young people. He was arrested and imprisoned. Released 20 days later, Kim found his young supporters waiting and another demonstration occurred.

From that period forward, Kim Young-sam came to take a place as a pivotal figure in the opposition to the authoritarian government and acted more and more as a leader of younger civilian politicians. Again in the sixth elections for the National Assembly, Kim won a seat and held various posts in the opposition during the next five years. Altogether he has been elected to the National Assembly nine times since 1954, elected president of the opposition four times, served as floor leader five times, and been spokesman for the opposition twice. It is a unique record in a country where regional, class, religious, and family feuds fractionalize the political spectrum, making it difficult to maintain coalitions and to sustain a relatively objective approach to contemporary political problems.

In 1969, the former army general Park Chung-hee was reelected president and attempted to institute the so-called Yushin (Revitalizing Reform) constitution. This led to an even more authoritarian rule, and Kim became one of its bitterest opponents. He announced that he would fight for the presidency in the 1971 contest. In 1970, however, he abandoned that idea after Kim Dae-jung, Kim Young-sam's longtime rival, became the opposition party nominee. Kim Young-sam loyally and enthusiastically announced his support of Kim Dae-jung and stumped the country backing his candidacy. And, it was in no small part due to Kim Young-sam's support and organization that Kim Dae-jung, the opposition standard bearer, was only narrowly defeated by Park in the 1971 election. This election was widely believed by Korean and foreign observers to have had many irregularities.

These two men—Kim Young-sam and Kim Dae-jung—have so dominated the political scene over the last quarter of a century that some Korean political observers have only half-jokingly referred to the recent period in Korean history as "the era of the two Kims". The two could not create a greater contrast. "Y.S." is something of an extrovert—often smiling, gregarious, a man who listens—his political collaborators say. But he is also a powerful leader, and one adviser close to him says his heart is strong and bold like a lion's. "Y.S" is fond of aphorisms. His favorite: "There is no gate on a main thoroughfare." By Korean standards—and, again, we are talking of a culture steeped in Confucian ritual and etiquette—"Y.S." is unconventional. It is seen as something of a novelty, and a badge of honor among his immediate assistants, that he generally carries his own briefcase. That is simply not done by most Korean executives, not in the private sector, and certainly not among government officials. His informal and unpretentious style is apparent in other ways, too. He is a jogger. The family home, not in one of Seoul's best neighborhoods, is relatively simple although recently refurbished. (On a visit, Henry Kissinger, Kim Young-sam's son recalls, recommended that Kim move into something more fitting his station in Korean politics.) One of Kim's two sons works closely with his father; the other is an independent businessman in Los Angeles. A daughter also lives in the United States.

Both Kim Young-sam and Kim Dae-jung have served

as lightning rods for opposition to the authoritarian regimes, first during the Rhee regime and then the military
governments which have followed. Both have suffered, as
a result, imprisonment and threats to their lives. "D.J"
was kidnapped from Japan back to Korea by the former regime. "Y.S." was attacked with acid by an agent of the Korean Central Intelligence Agency (K.C.I.A.). In other
times, when they were part of a united opposition to authoritarianism, Kim Dae-jung said, "There is a great deal
to be said about Kim Young-sam, but most of all I would
like to compliment him on his bravery, especially for his
determination to fight for democracy in this country. Not
only is he a firm and determined politician, but he also
knows how to embrace others, and that may be why he is
attractive to so many people."

The two are locked in a struggle for the presidency in
1992, in what seems to be the denouement for both of
them of their long political careers. Some Korean observers believe that it is the candidates' personalities which
will really decide the contest. The analysts argue that the
issues may be less important than the candidates' differences as personalities—given the nature of contemporary
Korean problems, their intellectual approaches, and their
limited options. This would be true, they contend, despite
the rivals' long competition and their very real differences
on issues.

After the Kims lost the fight to prevent Park's reelec-
tion, the next year the government rammed through a national referendum, after declaring martial law and
approving a new constitution. The new "Yushin" constitution greatly expanded the powers of the presidency at
the expense of the National Assembly. It also provided for
an electoral college for future indirect election of the president. With the promulgation of the new constitution,

Park declared a state of national emergency. Both Kims were overseas when word of Park's new usurpation of power reached them. Kim Young-sam was at Harvard University, a guest of the late Prof. Edwin O. Reischauer of the Harvard-Yenching Institute in Cambridge. A well known Japan scholar and formerly U.S. ambassador to Japan, Reischauer suggested to Kim that he might want to stay and teach for a few months until the situation in Korea became clearer. Kim says he will always be grateful for Reischauer's graciousness. But, he told Reischauer that he thought not. Instead, he traveled to Tokyo to learn further news of what was happening in Korea and then decided to return home to do whatever he could do within the confines of the new dictatorship. It is a decision of which he is very proud. He feels that he went back to take his chances with the Korean people rather than sit out the period overseas.

In 1975, Park issued Emergency Decree No. 9, banning a variety of political activities. As a result of the repressive measures, Park was reelected to another term in 1978. In May 1979, Kim Young-sam was elected leader of the New Democratic Party, defeating the previous leader Lee Chul-seung. Kim Dae-jung, released from house arrest by Park, expressed his support of Kim Young-sam as the leader of the united opposition. Remembering his old promises to do everything he could toward reunification, Kim Young-sam suggested publicly that he would be willing to meet in North Korea to talk about the possibilities of reunification, and the North Koreans responded by suggesting that a meeting be held between the North Korean Workers Party (The Communist Party) and the Kims' New Democratic Party.

Police raided the headquarters of the New Democrats in August to disperse a group of strikers who had been locked out by their company. The Seoul District Court, under pressure from Park, issued an injunction suspending Kim Young-sam as leader of the New Democrats, charging that he had been elected chairman illegally. Kim was dismissed by the government from the National Assembly. To protest Kim's dismissal, all 66 opposition members of the National Assembly resigned. That touched off rioting and demonstrations by students and Kim's supporters in Pusan and Masan. This occurred in southeastern Korea, Kim's power base. By October, students at the Pusan universities began demonstrations in favor of Kim Young-sam, their native son, protesting both his expulsion from the National Assembly and the *Yushin* system as well. Pusan citizens joined the riots which spread to the industrial city of Masan, scene of the original uprising against the Rhee government in 1960. Martial law was declared in the city.

In the midst of all this confusion, on October 26, 1979, Park and his bodyguard were assassinated in a plot led by the head of the K.C.I.A., Kim Jae-kyu, at a dinner party at his headquarters in Seoul. Kim Young-sam, who had predicted that something dreadful would overtake the country as a result of the increasingly oppressive nature of the regime, returned triumphantly to the National Assembly in November along with the opposition members who had resigned over his dismissal. And before the end of the year, in part through the mediation of Kim Young-sam, an interim government was set up through the electoral college with former Prime Minister Choi Kyu-hah as interim president to pave the way for constitutional reform and elections. Early in 1980, partly through Kim Young-sam's good offices, again, Interim President Choi restored the civil rights of Kim Dae-jung, former president

Yun Po-sun and another 685 dissidents identified under the Park regime.

But by May 1980, college protestors were in the streets again and had shifted their agitation from university reform to the broader national political agenda. Their demands included democratic elections, abandonment of the *Yushin* constitution, and objections to Gen. Chun Doo-Hwan serving concurrently as head of the defense security command and the K.C.I.A.—obviously a power base from which he could move to head the government. While President Choi was on a trip to the Middle East, massive but generally peaceful student demonstrations took place in Seoul—with as many as 60,000 students in the streets—and in provincial cities as well.

President Choi cut short his trip and returned with a promise from the cabinet to the students that he would announce a timetable for a return to democratic, elected government. But anti-government demonstrations continued and the interim government started a crackdown by ordering martial law nationwide. Decree No. 10 was issued, closing all universities and colleges, banning political activities and strikes, providing for prior censorship of all media, and prohibiting "slanderous statements" against government leaders.

This led to the Kwangju Incident—an echo of one of the earliest demonstrations of nationalist sentiment in the first days of the Japanese Occupation. Both events took place in that same provincial city. Student demonstrators in Kwangju called for lifting martial law and the release of their fellow regional native, Kim Dae-jung. Army special-forces teams were sent into the city and clashed violently with the demonstrators, with many students killed. That brought on a general uprising of Kwangju citizens, who seized rifles and vehicles from the military and took control of the city for nine days before the army could regain control on May 27. Military authorities closed the National Assembly and the headquarters of both political parties.

The violence in Kwangju had become the pretext for the Special Committee for National Security Measures, organized with Chun Doo-Hwan as its head, to take power in August 1980. This was a demoralizing reversal. After Park's death, it had been assumed that Kim Young-sam would contest the presidential election, and the end of Park's 18-year rule would introduce a new period when democratic government might be reinstated. The "Three Kims"—Kim Young-sam, Kim Dae-jung, and Kim Jong-pil (the head of a smaller opposition party)—seemed ready to compete for power in the elections. But again the violence that was so often to dog the Korean scene took over: Maj. Gen. Chun Doo-Hwan, defense security commander, took over the government in May 1980 in another *coup d'etat*, precluding the possibility of genuine elections and a return to democracy.

This fragile alliance did not hold after the tumultuous events of 1987; when students, joined for the first time by ordinary middle class Koreans, demonstrated in massive numbers for immediate democratic reforms in the upcoming presidential election. A complex combination of factors—including the split in the opposition, citizen demands for reforms, a constitutional requirement for President Chun to step down after his single term, and the surprise "Declaration of Democratic Reforms" by government candidate Roh Tae-woo—gave Roh victory in the election with only a plurality of votes among the four candidates. Almost immediately after his election, he began a process of reform that restored freedoms to the press, the labor unions, universities, and other social and political institutions.

It was events following the 1988 National Assembly elections, however, that proved Roh's own devotion to democracy and brought Kim Young-sam to the fore as a democratic leader, dedicated to forging the alliances necessary to lead his modern country. In the elections, the opposition parties got their first combined majority in the history of the Republic of Korea. Yet it quickly became clear that this historic event would not lead to a new era of collaboration, and the threat of a return to the old forms of government emerged in Assembly inaction that prevented the passage of legislation and stymied other parliamentary activity. Kim Young-sam recognized the need for revolutionary and dramatic change in this situation when he warned his colleagues in the now defunct Reunification Democratic Party on January 15, 1990, ''So long as you remain obsessed with the past, there will be no future for you.'' That was a hint that Kim was ready for a new alignment in Korean politics. A week later, he announced that his party had combined with the ruling Democratic Justice Party and the smaller opposition Democratic Republican Party to create a new grouping, the Democratic Liberal Party. This alliance had a two-thirds majority in the Assembly.

The move aimed at ending the 30-year monopoly of the Korean military on the presidency by creating a broad, centrist party with support among the former opposition and within the government bureaucracy as well as the military. It has not been clear sailing. The party faces not only the problem of welding the three former political groups together but that of fighting regional loyalties, which are among the most potent forces in Korean politics. Nonetheless Kim hopes to position the party away from the authoritarianism that has characterized all Korean governments in the past. Whether or not he wins the presidency in the December 1992 election, Kim's skills at political reconciliation have enabled a big step to be taken in moving Korea to a new level of political maturity.

Roh has rightly described Kim as "the pivot" of the new party. His experience with almost every political group in the country, through his 30 years as a prominent member of the opposition is invaluable. Kim's well-rounded background made him the natural choice for the new alliance. One of the negotiators who played a principal role in the historic compromise said that the thinking in political circles went something like this: Kim Jong-pil was ruled out. Negotiations revolving around Kim Dae-jung also proved fruitless. It was to "Y.S." that Roh turned for a solution because Kim was according to a source close to the negotiations, "a man who represented the legitimate conservatives of this country." Furthermore, "Y.S." was flexible and seemed to have the ability to run the country. He was a listener, a conciliator, and a skilled manager. "The process [of government], too, is important," the man who played the role of chief negotiator of the new alliance said. "The question of presidential competence boils down to leadership, rather than expert knowledge, a quality that is hard to define—but which Kim has," he concluded.

Kim says his decision to make a pact with the ruling party—and in reality with the military who had held power for 30 years—was a difficult one over which he mused for a long time. He had rejected the possibility of a coalition government which was offered first by Roh. Both, undoubtedly, had strong memories of the post-Rhee revolutionary period: Under Chang's effort to preside over a very diverse coalition, the country moved toward chaos. Although the threat appears to have abated somewhat because of the disintegration of the Soviet Union and the whole Communist Bloc as it had existed during the Cold War, the concern is that any kind of civil or political conflict inside the Republic of Korea will be exploited by the Communists in the North.

Kim believes his bitter fight during all those years for justice and high principle made him all the more sure of his decision when he made it. "History will always reveal the truth," he says, "and I believe in our people and their ultimate integrity. There is a limit to dictatorship. Had I not believed that, I would be dead now. That was why it was possible for me to organize, but be defeated over and over again. . . to organize, for example, our Democratic Alpine Society. . . It's why I could go on the hunger strike, even when I was under political restrictions set by the dictatorship." Another one of Kim's favorite sayings may be appropriate here: "Even if the rooster's neck is twisted, the sun will still rise at dawn."

By putting together a new party with elements of his old opposition and the government, Kim has managed to avert another crisis and to offer the country a stable, moderate alternative to the military-backed authoritarian rule. The military, many of whom genuinely see themselves as the last repository of sovereignty and as the defenders of the Republic, now have a sense of assurance that Kim Young-sam is the kind of moderate of whom probably a majority of the generally conservative Korean electorate approves. That confidence appears to exist even though the government will be in the hands of a former leading member of the opposition in the long struggle against authoritarian rule; but, of course, the final choice must be made by the voters in the December 1992 elections. Those voters now are offered the possibility of a clear choice between Kim Dae-jung's left-of-center politics and Kim Young-sam's moderate conservatism.

three

Managed from above, markets from below

The political decision of the voters in December 1992 coincides with an awareness by Kim Young-sam and Korean leadership generally, that the Korean economy is now at a crossroads. It is time for some major new choices and Kim believes he is the man to make them in The New Korea and in a new world environment.

Just as he is ready to move forward on the political plane to establish a new standard in elected government and democratic participation in Korean politics, the Korean economic establishment generally is ready to move toward new economic strategies to enhance and continue the fight for Korean prosperity. The reasons are clear: Beneath the Korean miracle are some deep cracks. The consumer price index has increased at almost double-digit rates for two consecutive years from 1990-92. The balance of payments returned to a deficit in 1990 after four years of surplus. And although the gross national product continues to climb nine percent as of early 1992, it is clearly moving above a sustainable figure for long term growth and thus feeding the inflation. This growth, furthermore, is being fed by consumption rather than by exports and investment.

The underlying causes of the new economic malaise in macroeconomic performance is based on a number of factors: Wages have increased too quickly, much higher than the increase in productivity, giving Korea the second highest labor costs in the region after Japan's. The democratization decree of June 1987 by President Roh unleashed a wave of wage demands and strikes. More than 3,000 "labor-management" disputes were reported in the next two years. The pattern of the disputes varied greatly. Some called for "democracy" in labor-management relations, some were intra-union, while others alleged discriminatory practices against blue-collar workers. But there is little doubt that the massive wave of work stoppages indicated a major turning point in labor-management relations in Korea.

All this diminished the comparative advantage of Korea, and thus Korean exports have slipped badly, especially in low-tech industries. On the technological front, as the comparative advantage of Korean industry shifts to the hi-tech sectors, the transfers of technology to begin to build a native research and development base inside the country are costly and difficult. Major industrial countries are increasingly reluctant to lose their own competitive advantage through technological transfers.

Perhaps most important for politicians like Kim, attention will have to be paid in The New Korea to the voice of interest groups with particular demands on the government and the economy. They now will constitute political constituencies. "Under former authoritarian regimes," Kim says, "the planners could adopt economic policy based solely on economic considerations, even when they were wrong. Now we have to arrive at a new consensus though a process of compromise and cooperation, a process for which there has never been a Korean tradition, and which takes place at the very moment in Korean and world economic history when those decisions have to be made quickly. It isn't going to be easy."

Kim and other leading Koreans who truly understand the nation's economy are more than aware that this adjustment is more than a difficult one. Many other countries at different times have simply been unable to make it. There is, unfortunately, no guarantee that the brilliant past of rapid economic growth can be carried on into the future. The only thing that the past does indicate is that Koreans have been successful in a period when many other countries have failed and that gives them a sense of confidence that they can take into the future in dealing with the whole range of new problems.

Furthermore, there is a completely new philosophy in the air: Even during the height of the government interventionist economic policies of the 1960s, Park Chung-hee often apologized for the government's extensive role. Government intervention as such has never been a precept although it has been a major tool for the past 30 years. Perhaps due to the profound anti-Communism of most of Korea's political class and the constant threat from the Communist North, Korean leadership is convinced that in the long run liberal economics and politics are preferable. "Now, with the collapse of the Soviet model," Kim says, "not only in the former Soviet Union itself, but in the more advanced countries of Central Europe as well, we conservatives have won the argument. Korean left-wingers can no longer ignore the failure of Communism in North Korea. That's why the prevailing mood in Seoul is for a liberalization of the economy as the roadmap for getting out of our current problems."

This consensus is reinforced by the large numbers of young Korean economists and managers who have returned from schooling and training overseas, particularly in the United States. This group of highly trained economists, managers, and technicians knows full well that the road ahead will not be a smooth one. The Republic of Korea will have to maintain a high rate of growth, further improvements in the quality of life, and more balanced regional development. All this will have to be done within the new structure of political democracy that Kim Young- sam and the rest of the opposition have fought for at such great personal sacrifice over the last 30 years. And, all this will have to take place as the economy is restructured for the increasingly integrated international arena in which it will have to compete.

"To build The New Korea's society, rapid economic development is one of the most essential pre-requisites," Kim Young-sam says. "Not only that, but we will also have to grow at a more rapid rate than other industrial economies, simply to provide the financial basis for developing a scientific base now required of a developed economy." There are other compelling reasons why Korea must continue its high growth rates if it is to succeed: Despite the current slower population growth (in 1992, it is about 0.91 percent), the working segment of the population will continue to grow because of the population explosion which has already occurred. Increasing numbers of jobs must be created to support past growth rates, and that will be more difficult than in the past as the economy moves away from labor-intensive manufacturing to more sophisticated industrial products. Always hovering in the background is the hope and the belief—but also the challenge—that sooner or later the Republic of Korea will have to incorporate a bankrupt North that has all the problems that a half century of Communism has inflicted on that population of some 20 millions.

Korea will not only face the challenges of competing with the older industrial societies in the new technological industries, but it will have to vie with the East Asian Newly Industrialized Economies (NIEs) for many of those same markets. To fund the development of these new industries in the 1990s, Korea will have to increase domestic savings and concentrate even more on the development of human resources.

Korea has maintained an enviable record among the developing Third World societies in achieving a relatively equitable distribution of income. But in a new more democratic political environment, income distribution will become an important point of discussion among competing constituencies. Nor have the intense regional rivalries in the Republic of Korea disappeared, and they are again likely to be intensified if and when the North is brought into the society. In fact, some observers believe that urban-rural, regional, and class disparities and rivalries are already on the upswing.

Again, as a representative of the majority population of the southeast, Kim Young-sam will have an important political as well as economic task before him. It will therefore be more necessary to take social and political factors into account in any economic planning and strategies in the future. "It is an argument that we have been trying to make, mostly unsuccessfully, to the government bureaucrats for thirty years," Kim says. "In the long run, having a balanced and equitable development program is the only way to have an efficient and continuing development program. And in the spirit of compromise and understanding, we now will have to find the way to do that in our institutions. I am extremely optimistic that we can manage it in our own special Korean way."

Liberalization of the economy will bring into play difficult politico-economic problems, opening up the issue of "injured" participants, particularly in agriculture and in the services. All of this will have to be wrapped into a package which will permit popular participation to an extent not known in Korean history. And, it will be made more complex if not more difficult by a population with rising educational and social standards. With that greater participation, decision-making is going to take more time just at a point when it ideally should be more responsive and rapid. The whole problem of interest groups—which are such a difficult issue in West European and American democracies—will introduce still other complications.

Yet there are reasons for optimism: Korea does not seem to be following in the pattern of some other rapidly developing economies, notably Japan, for whom a shortage of skilled labor may be their principle economic barrier. The population in the workforce will be growing throughout the 1990s. Their ratio to the total population is expected to rise from 59.3 percent in 1987 to 1991 to 62.7 percent during 1997-2000. Thanks to the growing propensity of Koreans to pursue education, the country will continue to build a large pool of increasingly skilled manpower. The reservoir of women, a very large number of them recipients of higher education, has only begun to be tapped. There is also, at least in theory, tremendous potential to raise the level of Korean labor productivity. Even though the efficiency of that resource has been climbing at ten percent annually over the past two decades, the potential for further increases has by no means been exhausted.

Korean workers, on average, will be young compared to those in the developed world; and each new generation is better educated than the one preceding it. In addition, the introduction of new technology should result in a continuing rise in the productivity of Korean workers. Furthermore, there is a possibility of an added pool of human resources developing if and when North Korea is incorporated into a reunited Korea.

How will these challenges of The New Korea be met?

Kim Young-sam, as well as most of the Korean economic and political leadership, understands that the level of interdependency around the world has intensified. Korea, with its long history of exporting even under Japanese colonialism, has a tradition of presence in world markets. The Korean War, the events which followed it, and Korea's alliance with the United States have intensified that global relationship. So there is no question in political circles that Korea is enmeshed in world economics and politics and must participate competitively to survive.

Given what are now recognized as the costs and benefits of authoritarian, centralized economic control in the country's recent past, and recognizing the worldwide movement toward market economics and away from socialist models; Kim and his advisers believe that the Korean economy must logically move toward further liberalization. Actually, since the early 1980s, Korea has taken a series of liberalizing measures including the opening of domestic markets to imports and the reduction of tariffs. Korea's degree of market opening has reached those of the developed countries with a current import liberalization ratio on manufactured goods of 99.9 percent and an average tariff rate of 8.4 percent in 1992. Thus liberalization of trade has been completed except in agriculture and services. The Korean leadership (like that of Japan, Taiwan, Mexico, Canada, and a host of other countries) would prefer to have the political protection of a multilateral, worldwide giant step in trade. Such a step would be provided by successful completion of the current Uruguay round of the General Agreement on Tariffs and Trade. The GATT negotiations are still being pursued under the aegis of the major powers. But (at the time of this writing) the deadlock in a fight principally between the U.S. and the European Community over farm subsidies obscures the outcome of that process.

The most difficult trade relationship for Korea is with Japan. Since the normalization of relationships between the two countries in 1965, there have been extensive trade frictions. They arise primarily from the Republic of Korea's chronic trade deficit with the Japanese. The accumulated deficit from 1965 to 1991 was $66.3 billion; in 1991 alone it was $8.8 billion, thus exceeding the total trade deficit of $7 billion. A troubling aspect for Korean economic planners is that the trade imbalance results from what they regard as the Korean industrial structure's growing dependency on Japan. The economic establishment in Korea believes that the way out of this problem is the upgrading of Korea's industrial competitiveness. That, they say, would require a smoother flow of technology from Japanese to Korean industry and a wider opening for Korean products into the Japanese market. An agreement to finance technological transfer from Japan to Korea, made two years ago, has not lived up to expectations. The problem may also require additional investment by the Japanese, even as minority equity partners in Korean industry. Japanese investment in the Republic of Korea during the period 1962-1990 totals about $3.8 billion, and is only at around the same level of U.S. investment of $2.3 billion.

Korea would be helped considerably if Japan were to further reduce the tariffs on Korea's main exports to Japan—i.e., textiles, footwear, and petrochemical products. But, these industries which are already in considerable difficulty in Japan pose a domestic political problem for the Japanese leadership. Despite the rhetoric, the relations between Koreans and Japanese always are tainted by the ugly past. Nevertheless, the Korean economic establishment is acutely aware of the importance of maintaining a close economic relationship for the benefit of both economies.

Despite the domestic political difficulties that it entails and if he is elected to the presidency in December 1992, Kim Young-sam says that he intends ''to continue full tilt at liberalization. There is no alternative but to continue moving forward that way.'' However, on the touchy issue of agricultural subsidies, Kim asks for additional time to make the adjustments. He also notes that the matter would be swiftly resolved if the General Agreement on Tariffs and Trade (GATT) round is successful. Liberalization of rice pricing, for example, which accounts for 62 percent of farm income in Korea in 1991, must be handled in such a way as to minimize the impact on farmers while they convert to other products.

In the area of invisible trade transactions, the government has already instituted liberalization measures in accordance with the International Monetary Fund's (IMF) Article VIII. Seventy-nine percent of the total investment areas were eligible for direct investment from 1991 and a final liberalization plan for the rest of the financial markets is now in place as well. The regime says it has a step-by-step approach to opening the capital market since it is argued that interest rates and exchange rates might not be able to absorb a full opening all at once. It is also contended that Korean domestic financial organizations must be strengthened in the meantime to enable them to compete at international levels. Kim Young-sam advocates freeing the central bank in a gradual process so that it may become an independent organization, modeled, his advisers say, after the U.S. Federal Reserve more than after the Bank of Japan with its more highly centralized organization.

Kim's advisers see the need to move to liberalize services as well, precisely because of what they anticipate will be growing international pressure to open services up to foreign competition. A reform of financial institutions would also be necessary in order to increase domestic savings to meet the increasing needs of the hi-tech, capital-intensive industries into which the country's manufacturing sector must move. They recognize that the service component of industrial activity will grow disproportionately in the period ahead because of the expanding use of information and communications available from new technologies. ''We feel that Korea should welcome this inevitable trend,'' Kim notes, ''and use it to our advantage. In many service industries, Korea's international competitiveness is being hampered by monopolistic control and overregulation, and that, again, is a reason for pursuing liberalization policies with greater vigor.''

According to present plans, external financial liberalization will proceed on schedules mapped out in the 1980s. An interest rate liberalization was announced in August 1991 and full implementation will take place in four stages. The first stage began in November 1991 and was completed in June 1992 with the freeing of most money instruments, including bankers' acceptances and large denomination commercial paper. Deposit rates for banks' large denomination certificates (CDs) and securities companies' repurchase agreements (RPs) were also among the rates liberalized in the first phase. During the second phase, which will extend through 1993, the government will deregulate all lending rates of both banks and non-bank financial institutions excluding policy loans and long-term rates with maturities over one year. In the third stage, scheduled for 1994-96, interest rates on policy loans and deposit rates with maturities less than two years will be deregulated. And, then, in the fourth stage, after 1996, all remaining restrictions on bank deposit rates as well as coupon rates for public bonds will be lifted.

The Koreans argue that internationalization of the financial sector and the freeing of capital markets will have to follow the deregulation of interest rates and exchange rates as well as their stabilization in order to prevent excessive capital flows in one direction or another. Otherwise, discretionary controls will have to be maintained. Therefore, the economic planners have decided that the stock market will be opened on a step-by-step basis. According to the guidelines announced in September 1991, foreigners were permitted to purchase Korean securities

beginning January 1992. There has already been considerable interest by Western investors in the opening Korean
markets. However, combined foreign ownership will be
limited to 10 percent.

The new regulations permit foreign ownership of 15
percent of total outstanding shares for any company listed
with the Korean Securities and Exchange Commission,
with a single individual or institution limited to 3 percent
of one counter. Some foreign observers have been extremely critical of the Korean government's progress toward capital market liberalization. "... [T]he capital
markets of South Korea are in desperate need of reform despite a decade of tinkering by the government," writes Ed
Paisley.[2] "... In late June [1992], however, the MOF [Min-
istry of Finance] took a step towards the free market when
it unveiled its interim reform program which includes the
relaxation of a number of important regulations over the
securities, corporate bond and foreign exchange markets.
But the most fundamental of reforms—deregulation of interest rates—has yet to be seriously implemented." Paisley
notes that "Critics say the [Ministry of Finance] is exceed-
ingly unlikely to give up its overarching command of the
local financial system or of companies' access to overseas
capital markets. For the local capital markets, that spells
trouble."

Perhaps the most important step to the speeding up
of the liberalization process was the government's revi-
sion of the Foreign Exchange Management Act in December 1991. According to the Revised Foreign Exchange
Management Act, the current positive system, whereby all
foreign exchange activites are initially deemed proscribed
except when stipulated otherwise, will be replaced by the
negative system which permits in principle all those activities except those specifically denied. The restrictions

on the foreign exchange concentration system will be eased so that debts and securities will be exempted from concentration and only registration will be required for nonresidents. Notification for capital transactions will be instituted replacing the former approval system.

Nowhere will the task of liberalization and renovation of the Korean economy be more difficult than in industrial restructuring. All observers agree this step is now necessary. One of the central issues is the Korean *chaebol*, the huge conglomerates often owned by a single person or family. These peculiarly Korean organizations, which in some instances resemble the Japanese prewar *zaibatsu* or the postwar *keiretsu*, have played a positive role in national development. They have, for example, improved product quality and taken the lead in technological innovation for hi-tech industries. Despite these contributions, however, the 40-odd Korean conglomerates (which can include many companies—sometimes more than a hundred) often dominate commodity and factor markets. They can also promote noncompetitive behavior, prohibiting a more natural division of labor. Most importantly, they can largely exclude the development of small and medium-size industrial enterprises. The concentration of wealth (the *chaebol 50* represent about 34 percent of the gross output in 1990) also provides a target for political discord during a period in which the Republic of Korea is trying to move to a stable representative government.

Kim Young-sam says he wants to remove any impediment to the growth of small and medium-size industry. His advisers have come up with a multifaceted program which would eliminate the abuses of the *chaebol* system but still preserve an important role for the *chaebol*, particularly in international competition. Kim intends to pursue policies which would reduce the proportion of bank loans that now go to the 30 largest companies in the country and to encourage 40 percent of all lending to be directed to small- and medium-sized companies. An exception would be made for loans to hi-tech firms so as to maintain their international competitiveness.

The importance of the *chaebol* in international competition is illustrated by what has happened in the worldwide semiconductor business. When the Samsung group announced it would enter this highly demanding field of technology in the early 1980s, most foreign observers were skeptical. It was believed that the Koreans had neither the technical skills nor the manufacturing facilities to become a player in what was a hotly contested international market. Today, Samsung is the world's fifth largest manufacturer of chips. When American, Japanese, and German semiconductor chipmakers recently formed two new alliances for the future production and marketing of computer chips, Michael Borrus, a political economist at the University of California, Berkeley, noted that an important reason for the changed competitive strategy was the aggressive entry of Samsung into the international memory chip market. The Koreans have invested between $4 billion and $5 billion in computer memory technology, Borrus said, and have taken 15 percent of the world memory market since they began production in 1987.[3]

Samsung has since decided to enter another hi-tech field with a half-billion dollar investment, producing the thin-screen liquid displays (LCDs) used in portable computers and other electronic gear. Three other Korean *chaebol*—Goldstar, Hyundai, and Daewoo—are also planning to enter this field. Western suppliers of raw materials have eagerly come to Seoul to sell their products. "[B]ut the South Korean LCD industry, nonetheless, has its work cut out. In addition to a relatively thin technology base, it faces difficult decisions in funding research and production of LCDs, and many analysts are skeptical of the ability of South Korean companies to compete with the Japanese."[4]

The government intends to pursue energetically the present anti-monopoly legislation now on the books. This might cause some of the *chaebol* to give up subsidiaries which they have acquired simply to be represented across the board in all industries. One of the ways of doing this would be to move gradually toward restricting the present system by which *chaebol* companies in the same group guarantee loans of its other members. Kim particularly wants the government to "jaw-bone" the conglomerates for more cooperation with small- and medium-sized industry, in order to help the smaller firms specialize and become more efficient. The government would also introduce measures to disperse excessively concentrated corporate ownership, at the same time looking for ways to introduce more efficient and professional management to the *chaebol* in order to enhance their efficiency and competitiveness.

After the bursting of the so-called bubble economy in Japan, in large part based on land speculation, Korean planners are particularly anxious to correct the unequal ownership of land and financial assets. This is to prevent a similar disruption in the Korean economy. The government plans to appropriately redefine the concept of non-business assets—especially land and other real estate—and enforce progressive property taxes for those assets. Kim and his advisers emphasize, however, that they must take a long-term view. The concentration of economic power must be addressed through a comprehensive long-term policy, not measures simply designed for short-term impact. The changes must be also made through suasion where possible. "To deal with this issue, we have to look at both preventing excessive owner concentration and the promotion of market competition," Kim believes, "Both are important in formulating policy."

Most observers of the Korean economy believe that the most critical item in Kim's economic program is the encouragement of technology. Today, only 2.6 percent of Korea's gross national product is devoted to investment in science and technology. This will advance to 3.5 percent by 1996, according to the present Seventh Five-Year Plan. However, research and development accounts for more than four percent of the gross national product in most of the advanced industrial societies. "Because Korea is trying to catch up, it should be spending more rather than less than the more advanced economies," Kim says. "Furthermore, the acquisition and transfer of research and development from the more advanced industrial countries is becoming more difficult to arrange and expensive to purchase all the time."

Kim believes that several things must be done to encourage a more rapid expansion of research and development: First, the target to expand science and technology to 3.5 percent of the economy by 1996 has to be strictly adhered to. That should be done through tax incentives and by extending greater financial assistance. Kim's advisers want to define more clearly exactly what the government's role in this effort should be, especially in those projects that require large external resources. But the general policy is to leave the profit opportunities to private firms. Taking note of what is happening, particularly in the international electronics market, government policy would also try to encourage cooperative efforts in research and development among private firms. Basic science-and-technology programs would mainly be carried out in university settings with the government supplying financial support.

In order to realize this research and development program, educational facilities must be further expanded. Kim Young-sam believes that a major step here must be the organization of a new, major university devoted to science and technology. It should be tied to specific industrial needs for trained personnel. Kim believes that the rate at which the Republic of Korea can develop technology in the next decade may be the decisive element in deciding whether the Republic of Korea can join the ranks of the developed nations. The primary emphasis of the Seventh Five-Year Plan has already been placed on new technology, the introduction of additional foreign technology, and the development of highly trained manpower. The evolution of an information industry will be crucial in this effort. Information industries have a high growth potential and are labor intensive, both of which are reasons for their high planning and financing priority.

"...[A] sense of crisis has been mounting. If the present price instability persists and the balance of payments deficit continues," Kim told a business audience in mid-summer 1992, "our nation's potential for economic growth will be exhausted in the next several years. Unless we place our economy back onto a healthy, robust path of growth, we cannot expect to achieve our three most cherished national goals—political democratization, national reunification, and joining the ranks of the developed countries. The problems that our economy faces are not of a temporary, passing nature. The fact is that our Republic now stands at a major turning point where the economy and the society must be reshaped into a new framework in

response to fundamental internal and external changes
...What our country needs is a new corporate culture
which is innovation-oriented.''

Summing up, there are three facets to Kim's program
for revitalizing the economy: "Economic democratization, price stabilization, and higher living standards." He
says this program can be achieved by abolishing much
government regulation and revitalizing the free markets.
"The government must pursue an active economic diplomacy," Kim says. "And there must be safeguards to prevent damage from monopolies and oligopolies." Kim
calls for holding price increases to three percent for three
years by restraining government expenditures and restricting the growth of the money supply. He says some
way must be found to stem real estate speculation. He
aims to turn the balance of payments around in two years.

Kim Young-sam, with his long background in opposition to former authoritarian Korean governments and his
intimacy with the problems of his constituents, is particularly concerned that future development must be more
equitable and touch more of the Korean people than in the
past. That must include an attempt to solve such basic
problems as housing. The nation's shortage of housing
has primarily resulted from the rapid population growth,
the emergence of the nuclear family, internal migration to
the urban sector, and the obsolescence of existing housing
units. The housing problem in the urban areas is further
complicated by the high population density and the rapid
increase in land prices. To solve this problem, the Seventh
Five Year Plan aims at increasing the housing stock by
500,000 units each year. The public sector will concentrate on the construction of smaller housing units.

"Maintaining balance and equity in national development is essential to making it more efficient and pro-

moting the well being of our people," Kim says.
"Increased educational opportunities, social security,
and housing would result in the expansion of the middle-
class and the protection of the livelihood of the under-
privileged. This is a new cycle for us—the opposite of the
circle of poverty, political instability, and increased poverty that dogged our past. If we improve our social situation, we will be providing an underpinning for stability;
and that stability, in turn, will help us to keep on growing
at a fast rate, which will, in turn, provide us with more
stability."

four

Korea at the center of Asia

The geography of the Korean Peninsula, jutting down as it does out of the continent toward the islands of the Pacific Ocean, has defined the nature of the Korean nation in the past and continues to do so even in the world of instantaneous communications and rapid transportation. The terrain is almost universally mountainous, although not high by the standards of mountains in other parts of Asia. It has a minimum of arable land, a climate of extremes, and limited natural resources—at least in the South. Those factors have made life hard for and demanding on its people. On the other hand, the peninsula's confines have drawn a perimeter and helped to produce a homogenous and culturally unified people, far more so than than those of Korea's Asian neighbors. But as a land bridge between two major neighboring civilizations, the Chinese and the Japanese, Korea has also served as a battleground for its neighbors through the centuries.

Even in the world of the 1990s, with all the vast technological changes that have taken place, the fate of Korean society is still to a considerable extent the product of these basic geographic factors. The Korean people trace their origins to the founding of the state of Choson in what is today northwestern North Korea. Many centuries before the Christian era, Korea's roots were established by the Yemaek tribe (related to the Tungusic people that inhabited the Shandong Peninsula in northern China and the Liaodong Peninsula in southern Manchuria). But the growth of the power of the Yen state in northern China and the subsequent Chinese Chin and Han dynasties pushed Choson further south into the peninsula, and finally destroyed it as a political entity about a hundred years before the common era.

In 313 A.D., the first of three indigenous Korean kingdoms that were to emerge finally ousted the Chinese from what had been Chinese colonies established north of the Han River and created the kingdom of Koguryo. The colonies had been a center of Chinese commerce, culture, and art. Toward the middle of the third century, Chinese pressure again forced the emergence of two more kingdoms— modeled on Chinese rule—called Paekche (in the southwest) and Shilla (in the east). Again, geography played a significant role in the creation of two rather than one regime because the mountain ranges separate the southern part of the peninsula along a north-south line. This regional divergence is perpetutated into modern times and politics, and—along with many other factors— it helps to explain the intense regionalism that still dominates the Republic of Korea's life.

The whole of the Korean peninsula was finally united under Shilla, in alliance with the Tang Dynasty in China, during the seventh century of the common era. Under the Shilla, and the subsequent Koryo and Chosun dynasties, Korea was a nominal vassal of the Chinese regimes next door from whom the Koreans borrowed to create their own unique cultural identity.

The Western name Korea was taken from Koryo (meaning land of high mountains and sparkling streams). From Chosun (meaning beautiful morning) comes the more poetic translation, ''land of the morning calm''. A Korean state maintained its independence until 1910 when it was incorporated into the Japanese empire. The unified Silla dynasty (668-932), followed by the Koryo (932-1392) and the Yi (1392-1910) gave the Korean nation cyclical periods of consolidation, a flourishing civilization, and then decline. It was under the 500 years of the Yi dynasty, however, that after a period of intense cultural activity under Emperor Sejong (1418-50), the regime and the country went into a long period of sterile stabilization and decline. The *yangban* aristocracy fought over exaggerated aspects of Confucian rituals, engaged in dynastic rivalries and court intrigue, concentrated Korea's land holdings and was celebrated for its tax evasion. Attempting to seal itself off from the outside, the kingdom suffered from economic stagnation and general corruption. Japanese pirates attacked Korea's coast in the 16th century. Korea became a ripe target for Western colonialism and of Japanese expansion with that country's growing modernization after its own forced opening in 1860.

In 1875, the Japanese forced an unequal treaty on Korea when China failed to come to Korea's aid. The Korean court then began a game of trying to play off one Western power against each other and against the Japanese. But the court itself split into camps advocating one external power against another. Finally, when the Japanese participated in a plot to assassinate the Korean Queen who had opposed Chinese-supported reform, the King turned to the Russians for protection. Moscow was attempting to expand the Russian Empire from the northern reaches of Siberia and the Maritime provinces on the Pacific into Manchuria and Korea.

Again when an internal reform movement threatened the court in 1898, and China responded with troops, Japan seized the opportunity to dominate the peninsula. After its victory in the first Sino-Japanese War of 1894-95 (a war ostensibly fought over the Korean problem), the Japanese established hegemony over Korea. The final blow to Korean sovereignty came with the Japanese victory over the Russians in the Russo-Japanese War of 1904-05. Moscow formally acknowledged Japan's ''paramount political, military and economic interest'' in Korea while the other European powers and the U.S. acquiesced. President Theodore Roosevelt saw Japanese dominance in Korea as a way to block a Russian advance into the Pacific, and as a quid pro quo for Japanese recognition of U.S. ambitions in the Philippine Islands. Japanese domination in Korea was officially sealed when Japan replaced the king with an underage princeling, and finally, annexed Korea in 1910.

Japanese rule brought about drastic changes in Korea. Theoretically the Koreans were, as subjects of the emperor, on an equal footing with the Japanese in Japan's home islands. In fact, Koreans were treated as a subject people in their own land. That became increasingly onerous as large numbers of Japanese immigrants were brought in to staff the government and to foster the nascent industrialization, especially in the North. After a group of Korean students in Japan in 1919 called for independence in what is known as the March 1 Movement, a series of demonstrations ensued throughout the country, and the regime improved the situation somewhat.

But as the Japanese became embroiled in their expensive and bitter war on the Chinese mainland in the mid-1930s, the colonial government moved to mobilize resources in Korea and tried to stamp out all opposition through a policy which nominally tried to assimilate the Koreans to Japanese culture. The Japanese police authorities established official *shinto* worship and recognition of the Japanese emperor as a divine. Koreans were recruited for the Japanese military. Korean students were forbidden to speak Korean inside or outside school, and in 1939 an edict pressed Koreans to adopt Japanese names. During the war years Korean-language newspapers and magazines were totally suppressed.

By 1941 the Japanese colonial regime had built up a significant industrial component in the Korean economy in pursuit of economic self-sufficiency for the Japanese Empire as a whole. But this had been done at the sacrifice of Korean interests. Korean-owned enterprises were discriminated against in several ways, including the terms of access to capital. An increasing number of farmers became sharecroppers, or had to migrate to Japan or Manchuria because of conditions on the land, as Japanese immigrants acquired it. As rice was increasingly exported to Japan, per capita rice consumption declined to half the 1912-16 level. Although other coarse grains were imported from Manchuria to feed the population, total per capita consumption of all foodgrains was 35 percent below the

1912-16 levels and probably did not represent a shift to other adequate foodstuffs.

It is against this background that Korean bitterness toward Japan and all things Japanese continues today. In a convoluted way, even though the two societies and cultures have a long and intimate relationship and share in the great wealth of East Asian culture, there appears to be little slackening in the hatred which young Koreans have for Japan and the Japanese. This remains true even though the Japanese and Korean popular cultures draw on each other and today's young Koreans have not known Japanese discrimination.

Kim Young-sam, with his own personal experience of Japanese oppression, acknowledges that attitudes today are sometimes emotional when it comes to relations with Japan. But he also complains, as do most Koreans, that the Japanese have still not accepted the depth of their complicity for Korean misery during the colonial period. Since Park normalized diplomatic relations in 1965, repeated blowups have erupted, usually over some new revelation or scandal from the colonial or wartime past. Important personages in Japan's ruling Liberal Democratic Party or a cabinet member have exacerbated the situation by defending Japanese actions during World War II.

A typical example of this phenomenon occurred in the spring and summer of 1992: Japanese and Korean newspapers unearthed the fact that so-called ''comfort women'' prostitutes were employed by the military during the war for Japanese troops. Initially, Japanese government spokesmen denied the charge, then denied that there had been Japanese government complicity, and', finally, when both these claims were refuted, denied that the women had been compelled to enter these roles. This latter assertion was challenged by some of the women who actually participated in the events of the period.

Japanese officials suggested that the so-called "comfort women" sought the jobs. Many of the 200,000 women in this regrettable circumstance died of disease or in the battle areas during the war. However, one Japanese survivor of the war said that he participated in dawn raids on villages to recruit women who screamed as they were dragged away from their children and loaded into trucks. The ex-soldier says they were promised factory jobs but instead were taken to brothels where they were forced to have sex with dozens of soldiers a day. Japanese government spokesmen have said that the Japanese government feels "deep remorse" over the "indescribable pain and suffering" the women endured but that "no document has been found to show that these women were recruited by force." The Korean government has demanded that the Japanese government do further research in the matter.

"Such an insincere attitude will invite anger and criticism from the relatives of 'the comfort women,'" the Korean government said. Some Japanese critics of the general attitude toward wartime behavior, including the largest national newspaper, *Asahi Shimbun*, have echoed the Korean criticism. The whole exchange between Korean politicians and Japanese government and political-party spokesmen ricocheted through the press of both countries. There were enough former eyewitnesses who commented or came forward that the subject was kept alive for weeks, without any real resolution.

From time to time in the post-World War II period, the Japanese government has made statements accepting responsibility for the actions of the Japanese military government during both the colonial period and World War II in Korea. But the Koreans believe they have never been comprehensive. And there has been nothing like the de-Nazification campaign that took place in the Federal Republic of Germany or the extensive payments which Germany made to Jews and other victims of Nazi terror, no matter where they are now located. Nor has there been an organized campaign in Japanese schools to acquaint a younger generation with the nature of Japanese occupation policies in Korea, China, and Southeast Asia during World War II. Japanese school textbooks, for example, have skirted most of the major historical and moral issues associated with Japan's aggression on the Asian mainland in this century. Again, this may be a deep cultural trait among the Japanese to neglect wherever possible those unpleasant realities that can be obscured by the rapid movement which Japan itself has taken away from its past. This reluctance of the Japanese to face up to the past has often resulted in agitation among the Koreans. This, in turn, has excited and revived old passion.

Kim Young-sam's position is that the Japanese government must once and for all make a complete accounting of the wartime period and reveal the whole record. It seems unlikely that such a policy would be undertaken by the contemporary Japanese political leadership. The Japanese population with no personal acquaintance or knowledge of the pre-World War II period feels no remorse for the actions of their parents and grandparents. Thus, whatever can be done and will be done, it seems unlikely that the basic animosity between Korea and Japan will disappear as an element in international relations in East Asia for many decades to come.

"I regret that," Kim acknowledges, "and I will do everything I can in my power to make it possible for Koreans and their neighbors to live together peacefully in this corner of Asia. I only wish our Japanese friends would meet me halfway.''

It was the defeat and the breakdown of the Japanese empire which brought on the catastrophe of the Korean War, the central event in recent Korean history. What turned out to be the last moment entry of the Soviet Union into the war in the Pacific in 1945 led to the agreement among the victorious allies at Potsdam in 1945 to jointly disarm Japanese forces in Korea. The peninsula was divided along the 38th parallel for that purpose, with Soviet troops occupying the northern half in order to fulfill this function only. The two sectors became areas of military occupation by the Soviets in the North and the Americans in the South. The division was intended by the United States to be a temporary partition to restore order. The departure of the 700,000 Japanese troops in Korea, their dependents, and the accompanying civilian functionaries left behind almost a complete breakdown in the industrial plant built during the colonial occupation.

Furthermore, there was a vast inflow of Koreans from abroad to the 16 million people estimated to be living in the country at that time. More than a million workers returned from Japan, 120,000 from Manchuria and other parts of China. At the same time, the population was exploding at a 3.1 percent growth rate. The situation was further exacerbated by the Japanese who flooded the country with increasingly worthless yen as they evacuated. Social unrest developed with work stoppages despite the vast unemployment. The South was plagued with electrical shortages when the North cut off power from the nationwide grid. And political agitation among the Koreans, including a significant minority fired with left-wing idealism, reached a crescendo as the United

States and its military were blamed for much of what had transpired.

Against the wishes of most of the Korean revolutionaries who had come back from exile, the United States went to the United Nations to request a five-year U.N. trusteeship and U.N.-administered elections for a National Assembly. When Moscow refused to permit U.N.-supervised elections in the North—where it had installed a regime under the Soviet army with a returned Soviet officer, Kim Il-sung—Washington went ahead with the establishment of the Republic of Korea in the South. Seoul on the Han River, an ancient seat of Korean rule, was designated the capital; Syngman Rhee, a long-time Korean refugee from Japanese rule who had lived in Hawaii, became president. Rhee had been elected president of the provisional government in exile which had been founded as early as 1919 in Shanghai. That action was immediately followed in the North with the establishment of the People's Democratic Republic of Korea under Communist auspices, a replica of the regimes that Moscow was then putting together in central and eastern Europe.

Despite these developments, the United States, in full-scale demobilization around the world, withdrew its military forces in 1949. And Secretary of State Dean Acheson publicly placed the peninsula outside the U.S. defense perimeter in East Asia in a speech before the National Press Club in Washington, D.C., on January 12, 1950. "Whatever this implied for future U.S. action, Acheson's statement and congressional action with regard to South Korea merely gave a political voice to a military voice that had already been established."[5] In fact, this exclusion of the Korean peninsula beyond the defense perimeter, as strange as it might seem later to most observers, had already taken place already earlier under none other than the U.S. Far East Commander, Gen. Douglas MacArthur, and the U.S. Joint Chiefs of Staff.

So when on Sunday morning, June 25, 1950, the North Korean armed forces launched an attack on the Republic of Korea across the 38th parallel, the action came as a political bombshell not only in Korea and the Far East but around the world. As formerly secret papers leaking out of Soviet archives are now documenting, Joseph Stalin and Kim Il-sung had taken Washington at its word. Between 1946 and 1949, the regime in the North—with the assistance of the Soviet Union—had been preparing for just such an attack. More than 10,000 young men were taken to the Soviet Union almost immediately after Soviet troops rolled into the North for military training and large numbers of ethnic Koreans from Soviet forces—including Kim Il-sung who was to be lifetime head of the regime— were transferred into the North Korean forces.

By June 1950, North Korean forces numbered between 150,000 and 200,000 troops and were organized into ten infantry divisions, one tank division, and one air division. Soviet equipment—including automatic weapons of all sorts, T-34 tanks and Yak fighter planes—had been pouring into the arms of the regime headquartered at Pyongyang, a capital of earlier northern Korean regimes. South Korea's army of 90,000 poorly trained and equipped men were quickly overwhelmed, and Seoul fell within three days. By early August, South Korean forces, down to less than 50,000 effectives, were hemmed into a salient on the southwest coast around the port of Pusan facing Japan.

Despite earlier pronouncements, the Communist invasion of the South was seen by President Harry Truman as part of the worldwide effort of the Soviets to expand the area of Communist domination, and eventually to threaten Japan, only 120 miles across the Tsushima Straits. Truman summoned his advisers and asked what they thought he should do. The U.S. action was immediate: U.S. air and ground forces were ordered into action against the North Koreans.

How could U.S. policy have made such a 180-degree turn? Prof. Nam Joo-hong probably identifies the main answer correctly when he says: "Barriers to a coherent U.S. security policy in Northeast Asia could be found in the U.S.' preoccupation with the Marshall Plan and formation of NATO...Internally, the Fair Deal economy called for cuts in defense spending, overseas commitments, and the armed forces (demobilization). By late 1948, the total U.S. Army strength had been reduced to half a million and defense spending had been cut from 38.5 percent to 4.5 percent. Thus, it became increasingly difficult for the U.S. military to relate its limited capability to foreign policy needs that were gradually expanding."[6]

Despite the early rout, by September 15 General Douglas MacArthur launched what would go down as one of the most brilliant tactical moves in military history by landing an amphibious force of Americans and South Koreans at Inchon on the northwest coast of the peninsula, severing the North's lines of supply from the Soviet Union and China. Within weeks, the whole course of the war appeared to have been completely changed, with U.S. and South Korean forces not only retaking South Korea but advancing on much of North Korean territory with the expectation that unification would be brought about *force majeure*.

But again, in October, there was a major reversal when Chinese "volunteers" poured across the Yalu River from Manchuria. They enabled North Korea to eventually reestablish itself over much of its former domain, and again pushed U.N. and U.S. forces in great disarray toward Pusan. Eventually superior American firepower (and poor Communist communications and supply dependent on the traditional Korean A-frame carried on the back of porters) held the "human wave" tactics of the less technologically adept Chinese at bay. And, eventually, a front was stabilized near the old boundary between the two Koreas.

From 1951 forward, the war then turned into a stalemate with bitter but inconsequential minor actions by patrols from both sides. Nonetheless, it was some of the most miserable combat in modern warfare's history. A war of attrition ensued that neither side seemed destined to win. On July 27, 1953, a cease-fire was finally signed at Panmunjon between the U.N. forces—including units from 15 countries—and the North Korean forces and their Chinese and Soviet allies.

An argument inside the U.S.-U.N.-South Korean camp over whether to use nuclear weapons ended with the dismissal of MacArthur as commander and great bitterness on the part of Rhee and many South Koreans with their conclusion that Korean reunification had been abandoned as an objective. Large numbers of North Korean and Chinese prisoners—some of whom went on to Taiwan—were released by the South Koreans rather than being repatriated as the North insisted. This was a fruitless effort by Rhee and Korean nationalists in the South to derail the armistice process.

The effects of the war were horrendous to the peninsula and the people, and the situation was of extreme importance in the worldwide geopolitical struggle between the U.S. and the Soviet Union and China. Hundreds of thousands of Korean soldiers and civilians were killed. The exact figure will never be known and could be as high as a million. Among the five-million Americans who served in Korea during the war, U.S. casualties totaled 140,000 with 33,000 killed in action and another 20,000 deaths from other causes. Most of the peninsula was reduced to rubble.

"But the damage wrought by the Korean war cannot be measured in material terms alone," writes Lee Ki-baik. "This is because the war forced the Korean people, long conscious of their ethnic unity, painfully to face the tragic reality that their nation had been partitioned and that hope for eventual reunification had become still more remote."[7] Among the South Koreans before the war, a considerable portion of the body politic was on the left or had been at most indifferent to Communism. The war changed that and most Koreans became avowed anti-Communists. More than two million North Korean refugees flooded into the South dispersing families with several million members.

On the broader world plane, the war ended any possibility of patching up the 1940s alliance between the Western allies and the Soviet Union and solidified the two world camps, seemingly including Communist China as an ally of the Soviet Union (although it also sowed the seeds of the later Moscow-Peking split). "Korea" became synonymous with the great divide that had descended over Europe and the world. American troops were permanently stationed in Korea. Japan, toward which the U.S. had had ambivalent policies under the U.S. Occupation until 1950, not only profited from the rebuilding of its industrial machine during the war; but it became an ally of the U.S. in East Asian politics with Washington anxious to help redevelop its economic potential as part of the mobilization against the new enemy, world Communism.

five

The dream (and the reality) of reunification

Visitors to North Korea today find the quintessential Stalinist state. Pyongyang, the North Korean capital is (to mix Russian metaphors) a "Potemkin village"—a modern, well-designed city. But, its streets are largely empty, its government-rationed stores stock a minimum of basics, and its population is sullen and obviously repressed. A campaign to restrict North Koreans to two meals a day was still going on in 1991, and North American ethnic Koreans who had been in the countryside reported evidence of malnutrition.

It appears as though the whole country is in some

kind of time warp, lodged somewhere earlier in a decades-old Stalinist mold. Pyongyang and those environs which a foreign visitor are allowed to see appear to be a stage setting for Orwell's *1984*. Big Brother, the Great Leader Kim Il-sung, is everywhere. He stares down at passers-by from gigantic statues. His face is rendered in huge, realistic Soviet-style portraits. His nostrums about the good life under *juche* (self-reliance) are written out in huge *Han'gul* characters on banners hung across the broad streets everywhere. (The North has abandoned all Chinese characters in order to assert its nationalism.) The single television channel devotes long hours to the Great Leader. The audience sees images of a large, aging, nondescript Korean man in diverse roles and settings: smelling the flowers of his garden, meeting folk dancers from Bulgaria, or simply speaking to the numerous delegations of "the people" who call on him.

"Security" reaches the same exaggerated and ridiculous extremes it always does under totalitarian regimes. Riding down one of the main thoroughfares of the city, guides refuse to tell visitors the name of the street. Why are there no bicycles in Pyongyang? The answer: The Great Leader does not like bicycles. (Bicycle traffic makes the omnipresent surveillance of the secret police more difficult.) Energy shortages can be severe and can even stall public transportation. But, if one tries to photograph the long lines waiting for the Soviet-style electric trolleys stalled because of a severe energy shortage, the secret police will likely pop up to warn you off.

There are no signs of "the thaw" which began at least a decade ago in the Communist countries of Europe and which finally led to Gorbachev's *perestroika* and *glasnost* and ultimately to the collapse of the whole Communist system. North Korea's central rationale is that its

strategies and policies are immune to the shattering trans-
formations taking place in the rest of the former Communist Bloc. In a new twist, North Korea now believes it lives
by its own ideology, not according to Marxism-Leninism.
(For years, its propagandists had bragged about their own
faithful version of the latter faith).

Now, North Korea claims its path is free of the vagar-
ies that have overtaken the other Communist countries of
Eastern and Central Europe or even Communist China for
that matter. None of this leaves much room for discussion
or latitude for negotiation as Washington, Seoul, Tokyo,
and, perhaps, even Beijing try to defuse one of the last
powderkegs in the Cold War.

Nonetheless, the collapse of the Communist regimes
in Europe—and most importantly of all, the reunification
of Germany—have impacted heavily on North Korea.
Trade with the former Soviet Union has been put on a
dollar-and-cash basis. And, the economic breakdown in
the former Soviet republics reduces what North Korea can
buy and sell even further under these new terms. A former
Communist country's diplomat living in Pyongyang said
he had virtually no access to either North Korean officials
or, of course, to the general citizenry. In fact, representatives from the former Communist states get even worse
treatment than some of the non-Communist missions
from such countries as India.

The reason is clear: Moscow has turned its back on
North Korea by establishing full diplomatic relations with
Seoul. South Korean President Roh Tae-woo and Soviet
President Mikhail Gorbachev met in a summit in San
Francisco on July 7, 1990, under U.S. auspices, in an ef-
fort to begin to settle questions about the Korean penin-
sula. These questions had endured ever since its division
after World War II. The meeting was followed by Roh Tae-

woo's visit to Moscow in December 1990. Full diplomatic ties between the nations were established in October 1990 (along with ties to most of the former Communist states in Central and Eastern Europe).

Now almost completely dependent on China as its only ally, that bond has also been strained if not broken. For years, Beijing had threatened to veto South Korea's admission to the United Nations. In 1991, the P.R.C. refused to do so any longer. Indeed, Seoul already had a trade mission in Beijing—an embassy in all but name. As a result, Pyongyang had to swallow the joint admission of the two Koreas to the United Nations. It was, in fact, a stratagem long ago proposed by the South but vehemently opposed by the North.

In the 1980s, Soviet thinkers often drew an analogy between the Soviet and South Korean economies. Here was a superpower comparing itself with a second-tier, newly-industrializing country: not the U.S., West Germany, or Western Europe. . .but South Korea. The reason: South Korea had successfully entered all the industrial fields in which the Russians had been left behind—shipbuilding, automobiles, heavy chemicals, and, most importantly, electronics.

What other reasons stood behind the Soviet fascination? Czarist, imperial Russia's long-standing interest in the Korean peninsula perhaps prompted Gorbachev and his advisers to see Korea as a natural trading partner. Moscow may have also felt that South Korea could adjust to the Soviets' lagging level of industrial competence. Third, a working alliance could offer the Soviets opportunities in a new balance of power game in East Asia. Another dimension was added in 1989: A united Germany owed the Russians a debt for their reunification. Likewise, wouldn't a united Korea have a similar debt? The reunified country could become an even more important economic and political partner.

If this was Gorbachev's strategy; it got caught up, of course, in the general chaos which his radical internal reform loosed on the Soviet Union. The British newsweekly *The Economist* sums up the importance of a Russian rapprochement with South Korea or a reunited Korea this way: "[t]he growth of Japan and the Asian dragons is tipping the balance of economic power eastwards to the Pacific rim. Russia should therefore be seeking to develop its closest ties there. This is especially true because the Asian dragons are the countries nearest to Russia's own far east and its raw materials, and their technology is relatively unsophisticated, like much of Russia's. They also have experience of effective state intervention (and of lessening it) in a market economy."[8]

By the summer of 1992, South Korean enthusiasm for this new found friendship had abated somewhat. Kim Young-sam, one of the first Korean politicians to make contact with the Moscow leaders, says, "We, of course, want to become friends with the former Soviet republics, and I have no doubt that we can do business together. We have already shown our bonafides by extending a very large commercial credit."

Furthermore, Kim says, there are political games afoot. "The Russians are still one of the biggest players in East Asia and we need their cooperation to insure peace and stability in this part of the world. But we must proceed cautiously; unfortunately, with all our success, the Republic of Korea is not yet capable of bailing out the Russian economy—we can only do our share."

South Korea originally planned to extend the former Soviets $3-billion in credits over three years. But, initial shipments of $600 million in commodities have resulted already in default on Moscow's debts. Plans are also going forward for cooperation with Khazakhstan. (Stalin had relocated ethnic Koreans there to move them away from "sensitive" areas on the border of Japanese-occupied Korea.) But these plans may also now be awash in the widespread turmoil that has overtaken the former Soviet Union. With the degree of trouble in their economy, the Russians face the temptation of selling weapons to both the Chinese and the North Koreans. In the final analysis, Moscow-Seoul relations may be decided on the issue of whether the Russians can retain the influence to help move the North Koreans toward real negotiations for stabilizing the peninsula.

This continues to be an extremely difficult problem. Since the end of the Korean War, the Korean peninsula has been one of the most heavily armed areas in the world. It remains a major confrontational point between the world's two most powerful military forces—the remnants of the former Soviet Union and the United States. The Democratic People's Republic of Korea (North Korea) is the classic Communist militaristic dictatorship. North Korea in 1992 maintained a total of 995,000 uniformed military personnel, outnumbering the South by a ratio of over 5- to-1, and this does not include as many as a million more in reserves. To provide perspective, the North's population is less than half as large as the South's. The forces are organized into 16 corps commands with a special force numbering 100,000 men. Both its mechanized, self-propelled heavy artillery (built in North Korea) and its tanks have tremendous capacity for a blitzkrieg type offensive, according to Tong Whan Park, a member of the Korean Institute for Defense Analysis in Seoul.[9]

Park says that North Korea is known to have deployed

large stockpiles of chemical and biological weapons. More recently, the North Koreans sold and shipped new, improved versions of the Russian SCUD missiles to both Syria and Libya. The weapon, which was a terror device used against Israel and Saudi Arabia in the Gulf War in 1989, now has longer range and improved guidance systems. (It has been reported in some quarters in the U.S. that China supplied these systems to the North Koreans.)

The South Korean armed forces stand at 650,000— including 60,000 naval and 55,000 air force personnel. The forces are set up defensively across 11 corps commands, including the Capitol Defense Command, and maneuver corps. (Unfortunately, almost a quarter of South Korea's population lives in the greater Seoul area, which is within artillery range of the aggressively deployed North Korean forces.) Park says that the North has a quantitative edge in troops and weapons in all services, having begun a modernization program in 1962, twelve years before Seoul did. Park estimates that North Korea's militarized regime uses 48 percent of its defense budget for actual buildup. In comparison, the South has only 20 to 40 percent of its defense expenditures actually going into capital equipment because of such costs as land expenditures. Pyongyang is devoting as much as 22 percent of its gross national product to the military, Park believes, while Seoul's corresponding figure is only 4 percent. One must, however, take into consideration that the South's gross national product is ten times that of the North, making its actual defense budget about twice that of Pyongyang's. That will increase as the South Korean economy grows, while the prospects in the North are for a diminishing gross national product for the foreseeable future. That reality could persuade the North Korean leadership that time is not on their side; and that, if they are to use the military strength they have been building for years, it may be now or never.

Whatever the strategic value of Korea in the immediate post-World War II period when its role was initially denigrated by American strategists, the importance of the Republic of Korea has taken on new weight with the development of Japan, as an economic superpower, and South Korea's own technological and economic advance putting it on the threshold of becoming a developed industrial economy. "We had hoped that the collapse of the central power in the former Soviet Union would diminish the threat of violence here in Korea," Kim Young-sam says. "And there is an argument for that. But, unfortunately, there is growing evidence that Korea will remain a center of geopolitical struggles, precisely because the duality of world conflict has now broken down into multiregional theaters of hostility."

The reasons for this continued high profile of the Republic of Korea in any attempt at building the new world order are essentially three:

1. If and until the regime in North Korea transforms itself into a more stable, peace-loving state, or that regime collapses and Korea is amalgamated into a united country; there will continue to be a flashpoint on the peninsula between the two Koreas. The U.S. is committed to the Republic of Korea's defense. For the foreseeable future, it appears that American forces will remain in the South as a "trip-wire" to prevent new adventures by the North.

Furthermore, Pyongyang keeps the peninsula at a fever pitch anticipating war, not only by its propaganda, but by the actual disposition of its forces. "Ever since it announced it was ready for war in April 1970, North Korea has kept an overwhelming offensive posture by putting its forces on a hair-trigger alert along the front lines," Kim Young-sam says. "The North Korean forces are such that they can be moved without being detected by sophisticated U.S. military intelligence equipment. In addition, the North has numerous advantages over the South in making war. It has a war-oriented economy. It has dispersed its industrial activity for military purpose. And everywhere in the North, the Communists have built underground shelters and so forth. Unlike the North, we live with a defensive mentality that has shaped the whole course of our recent political and military history." Kim says, "Like most democracies, that makes us vulnerable."

The threat from North Korea has taken on new significance with widespread speculation in South Korea, the U.S., Japan, and Western Europe that Kim Il-sung has embarked on a search for nuclear weapons. North Korea has a substantial nuclear program with one major site at Yongbyon, about 60 miles north of Pyongyang. One component is a small reactor of about 30-megawatt capability which is able to produce about seven kilograms of plutonium annually. Another larger reactor is capable of yielding enough weapons-grade plutonium to arm as many as five nuclear weapons a year. There is some evidence that North Korea may have hidden nuclear sites, such as Iraq had before the Gulf War.

North Korea signed the Nuclear Non-Proliferation Treaty in 1985. However, until the summer of 1992, it refused to accept the safeguard requirements for inspection of its nuclear facilities by the United Nations International Atomic Energy Agency (IAEA) in Vienna. This was an unconditional treaty obligation, and the inspection is a critical first step—if only a first step—in eliminating the danger of nuclear weapons proliferation on the Korean Peninsula.

Pyongyang has been off-and-on in its negotiations to permit international IAEA inspection of the sites, arguing for preconditions. The first IAEA inspection has not yet convinced strategists in South Korea and the U.S. that activity toward producing nuclear weapons is not going forward. Such site inspection is limited to canvassing only what they are shown by signatories of the non-proliferation treaty. Consequently, there will be a continuing fear in Seoul and other capitals that, as in the case of Iraq, weapons facilities might go undetected.

2. The Korean peninsula is crucial to the stability and defense of Japan. While superpower confrontation may disappear, regional tensions will continue or grow. As the economies of the Republic of Korea and Japan become more and more interdependent, their strategic relationship also becomes more intense.

3. A school of thought has always existed that Beijing's hand was forced during the Korean War. Documentation for that case has been lacking but may yet appear from Soviet archives. China, it has been argued, came into the war after the strategy been plotted by the Soviets and Kim Il-sung's regime. Only when initial attempts failed to swamp the South Korean regime and when MacArthur's advance toward the Yalu River threatened to install an anti-Communist Korean regime on the Chinese borders of Manchuria, did the Chinese intervene. While this position has some validity, Chinese military power— enhanced by its nuclear weapons and missile technology—will remain a continual element in the calculations of any government in Seoul, no matter how much its relations may improve with Beijing.

"We Koreans in the South have always looked to the example of the formerly divided Germany as a model for what could happen on the Korean peninsula," Kim

Young-sam says. "But the analogy may not hold. The German Democratic Republic's fate was sealed when Moscow refused to support the East German hard-liners in their efforts to smash growing internal opposition. Then East Germany's economy began to collapse after serving for decades as the main transmission belt for technology from the West to the Soviet Union. But in the past, Moscow had given the East Germans orders—that has never been true for Pyongyang."

The question now is whether North Korea's Kim Il-sung will have enough flexibility to transform his own hardline regime to meet the rapidly changing world balance of power. Furthermore, he has personalized the regime as no Communist head-of-state has been able to do since Stalin's time. One can seriously raise the question: Will there be a second ruler of the North Korea he and his Soviet mentors created in the 1950s? For decades, students of the North Korean regime have exhaustively studied the few details that came out of a closed society and tried to understand how Kim Il-sung built an artificial aura around his name and his role. In a biography published last April, the North Korean dictator has begun to make admissions which belie some of the earlier glowing biographies. A hint now exists that his legendary role as an anti-Japanese revolutionary may have been exaggerated, to say the least—something long known outside North Korea.

But, as Clayton Jones has written, "Fiction or not, the official past of Kim Il-sung is everyone's present in North Korea. . . . [A] new theme can be found in the autobiography: Kim implies that his tactics of revolution may not be appropriate for the next generation, although the goal of revolution should be the same."[10] Koreans, undoubtedly on both sides of the Demilitarized Zone, are grasping at this straw. Now that Kim Il-sung is 80, they hope that he may be willing to change his strategy and tactics to preserve a place in history. The question remains whether Kim and the regime can make the changes necessary to accommodate the new world order without encountering serious problems...and, most worrying to the South Koreans, whether whatever happens in the North will not upset the delicate balance and the peace and stability now enjoyed on the Korean peninsula and in East Asia generally.

Reunification is the stated aim of both regimes, and is undoubtedly what the Korean people, North and South, would wish. But the two Koreas have historically approached the issue of reunification in quite different ways: The North has always insisted that reunfication must come about through an "independent" solution by the Korean people "by any means", hinting that it could still entail military might despite the bitter experiences of the Korean War. Pyongyang has always insisted, therefore, that the withdrawal of U.S. forces in South Korea would be the sine qua non of any movement toward reunification.

Kim Young-sam, throughout his political career, has been in the forefront of those advocating reunification of the country, an issue on which all Koreans, whatever their politics in the South, and whether they live in the North or South, appear to agree on in principle. But he believes he cannot base his hopes on prospects of a reunited country in the near term. The South always has maintained that peace must be maintained "at any cost," even if that means continuing national division. Pyongyang sees reunification as something that must be undertaken immediately while Seoul has always regarded it as a step-by-step procedure. Furthermore, the German experience of the past two years has come as a cold shower for most South Koreans who believe that they could have many of the same problems if their relatively prosperous South were, somehow, to absorb a North Korea impoverished by a 45-year militaristic Communist regime.

Unlike the former Soviet Union in the case of Germany, no major powers in the region are in a position to unilaterally or collectively impose reunification on the two Koreas. Recent visitors to Pyongyang believe that the North Korean leadership now understands that they are increasingly isolating themselves by living in a different geopolitical world. At the same time, this awareness has exacerbated their fear that South Korea's "indirect approach" to reunification is a conspiracy. South Korea's active pursuit of better relations with North Korea's former two patrons, Moscow and Beijing, in what Seoul calls *nordpolitik* (after the German *ostpolitik*) only adds to that paranoia. North Korea retreats into what generally has been traditional Korean thinking—with considerable justice—that Korea has simply been a victim of international great power politics since the middle of the nineteenth century.

Kim Il-sung apparently hopes to use the issue of reunification inside South Korea, as it moves toward democratization, to work up anti-American sentiment. He wants to achieve the first aim of his strategy which is to oust U.S. forces from South Korea. That policy is perhaps based on a misperception of the past history of political agitation against the authoritarian military governments in South Korea. Such agitation has increasingly failed as the administration of President Roh Tae-woo has become more liberal. Kim Young-sam, as Korea's first civilian president in thirty years and heading a broad alliance of former members of opposition and ruling parties, would have an opportunity to lift the issue of the terms of reunification out of the domestic debate.

Kim's and the South's hands have been strengthened most recently by a joint U.S. and Japanese statement on the occasion of a state visit by Prime Minister Kiichi Miyazawa to the United States. In fact, there was never any real concern about Washington's policy; but a statement was issued that neither Tokyo nor Washington will move further toward any kind of commercial ties with North Korea until the problem of nuclear inspection is resolved. There had been concern in Seoul and Washington that, responding to the pressure of Japanese business interests, Tokyo was inclined to help bail North Korea out of its present economic disaster. Some Japanese commercial camps are wary of a united Korea as a potentially formidable rival for third markets around the world—particularly in those labor-intensive industries which, again because of new competition from other areas of Asia and Mexico, are in trouble in Japan.

Pyongyang, in its turn, has proposed to Seoul a "Confederal Republic of Koryo". Despite a constantly changing emphasis on what the proposal actually means, it is clear that it envisages the end of the South's present anti-Communist regime. The South sees any such agreement as an interim recognition of two regimes within one nation, much like the two German states lived with after the end of the Hallstein Doctrine as Bonn tried to prevent international acceptance and recognition of the Pandow regime. Kim Il-sung sees this as a perpetuation of the division of the country. The rationale for the military regime and the economic sacrifice it has demanded of the people in the North has been the reunification of the country "at any cost". With the breakup of the Communist Bloc, longtime observers believe it will be harder than ever for Kim Il-sung to abandon that goal. To do so would require at least a gradual modification of the regime. The experience in Central and Eastern Europe has shown that process would be difficult at best without bringing about the collapse of the government itself. Further, the Chinese Communists apparently believe such modification cannot take place without the abandonment of the Communist Party's monopoly on power.

In July 1992, President George Bush announced that all tactical nuclear weapons had been withdrawn from South Korea and adjacent waters. It was a bold stroke aimed at reducing world tensions and appeasing a growing U.S. constituency that seeks to reduce the cost of the far-flung American presence around the world. This step followed the announcement a year earlier that all land-based tactical nuclear weapons were being brought back from overseas. Washington's move defuses North Korea's longstanding demand for a nuclear-free Korean peninsula. Seoul and Washington appear now in a position to call North Korea's bluff—a bluff manifested in the repeated statements and leaks from Pyongyang that it would permit international inspection of its nuclear facilities in return for "denuclearization of the peninsula." In midsummer 1992 there were also unofficial reports from North Korea that Pyongyang was now willing to give up its demands for a total withdrawal of American forces as a precondition for serious negotiations with the South.

Perhaps the most critical and unpredictable issue— and the one most puzzling to observers in Seoul, Washington, and Tokyo—is the question of the leadership in North Korea. Although Kim Il-sung is said to be in reasonably good health, he is 80 and has headed a regime during its entire existence. By whom or how would he be succeeded? Indeed, will it even be possible to find a new leader or leaders? "Looking at the leadership positions in the WPK (the Workers' Party of Korea, the ruling Communist Party in North Korea), one is struck by an extraordinarily high turnover rate," writes B.C. Koh. A large number of "Central Committee members failed to be re-elected at each congress. . .The turnover rate was equally high at the politburo level. . .It should be noted that the turnover rate in WPK's party organs has always been high; the practice did not begin with the rise of Kim Jong Il [Kim Sung-il's son and presumed successor]." Koh concludes: "If its economy continues to stagnate, the legitimacy of Kim Jong Il will remain fragile at best."[11]

Given the growing isolation of the North Korean regime, more optimistic observers hope Kim Il-sung might finally be ready for serious negotiations to reduce tensions on the peninsula. The forces which could bring this about are North Korea's difficult economic straits, the succession issue, and the growing industrial strength of the South. This strength will eventually be felt in the production of armor as well as civilian goods. In some quarters there is particular hope that the difficult economic straits of the North Koreans will force a new rationality in their policies.

There is some evidence that that is happening. Robert A. Scalapino, one of America's most prominent Asian scholars who has visited North Korea and who tends to look on what is taking place more optimistically than many, still has severe reservations: "While DPRK leaders have given faint signals for some time that they are aware of the present economic deficiencies, most efforts to encourage joint ventures and other forms of foreign economic intercourse have had very little result. The DPRK economy is currently in bad shape. Foreign debts cannot be paid. Growth is low and may have even been negative in the recent past. Plants are obsolescent, labor productivity is low, and living standards poor. New approaches cannot be long postponed, and the efforts to 'turn out' to the market economies, starting with Japan, seem certain to be accelerated. But can this be done without risking 'spiritual pollution'? Thus politics presently serves as a barrier to 'new thinking' in the economic realm. . . . Moreover, if political retrenchment in the USSR becomes a major trend, with 'law and order' the commanding imperative, the impact upon Asian Leninist societies may be substantial.''

But Scalapino continues: ''. . . [T]he period ahead promises to be a time of extraordinary, often unexpected, changes . . . .''[12]

Some movement has already begun along these lines with the South Korean *chaebol* looking at the possibilities of doing business in the North. Kim Woo-chong, the intrepid South Korean businessman who since 1967 has built Daewoo into one of South Korea's biggest companies with total sales of over 18 trillion *won* ($24 billion) in 1991, has been flirting with Kim Il-sung since January 1992. Kim Woo-chong followed in the footsteps of Chung Ju-yung, the head of Hyundai, South Korea's No. 2 *chaebol*, who had proceeded him. Apparently no firm deals developed. (Meanwhile, Chung had become a Ross Perot-like figure, entering the presidential sweepstakes as an independent candidate. With no previous political experience, Chung is expected to withdraw in much the same fashion as Perot did.)

Nevertheless, Daewoo's Kim says he hopes to move antiquated machinery from South Korea to the North, use North Korean cheaper labor, and export to markets which the Koreans are now losing to lower cost competitors in other developing countries—not the least of which is

China, just across the Yellow Sea. (Chinese exports of $71.91 billion passed South Korea's in 1991 for the first time by a sum of $40 million. In large part, this trade was in goods competitive with the Republic of Korea's former export successes.) A recent comparative survey of sales of foreign products in the American market made by KO-TRA, the Korean government export promotion agency, showed that the Chinese had taken markets from the Koreans in at least 15 different items.

"I am afraid that the past shows North Korea is prone to base its negotiating strategy on military power, alone," Kim Young-sam observes. "For example, because they are aware of our defensive military posture and our relative military weakness, they demand the withdrawal of U.S. forces in the South as a precondition for negotiation. Maybe some people, at first glance, believe that is a reasonable demand which would facilitate the solution of the military deadlock. The trouble is there is no guarantee that unification on these terms would be achieved in a 'peaceful' manner."

For all these complicated reasons, Kim Young-sam and the vast majority of political leadership in the Republic of South Korea want American forces to remain in the country as proof of the U.S. commitment to a free and prosperous Korea. They believe it will also guarantee that either the North will approach the issue of reunification in a peaceful step-by-step fashion or the South would be able to wait out the issue as it builds a more stable and prosperous Korean culture in its half of the peninsula.

The consensus in South Korea is that Kim Il-sung and North Korean leadership believe an American withdrawal would so unnerve the South Koreans as to make them ripe for North Korean blackmail or aggression. Such a withdrawal had been proposed by the Carter administration in the late 1970s but was defeated by the combined pressure of conservatives in Congress and the U.S. military.

Kim Young-sam hopes that a way out of the present impasse may be to move the whole peninsula toward some sort of arms control to lessen the threat of war. The North Koreans have made or hinted at modifications in their previous policy since 1988. On December 13, 1991, the two Koreas signed an historic agreement regarding reconciliation, nonaggression, and mutual exchanges. Yet it now appears that the document was merely a propaganda device and not intended for actual implementation. And Kim reminds non-Koreans that past North Korean propaganda initiatives have been linked to actual *increases* in armaments or in the forward positioning of their forces.

Kim Young-sam will continue to propose to the North Koreans that the two Koreas move forward in a series of confidence-building measures. None of them in themselves would be conclusive, but they would guarantee the security of both regimes. Some of the measures were used in the lengthy period of detente between the superpowers and are therefore tested. They would include the institution of a "hot line" between the two political chiefs and a credible system of arms-control measures. There would also be programs to improve contact and communication, among them the ongoing family reunification procedures and meetings between parliamentary groups. All these steps would help lessen the existing tensions. These measures would be capped with a nonaggression pact between the two Koreas and a final peace treaty ending the Korean War.

left: Kim Young-sam, who as a high-school student said he would be president of Korea, may well reach his goal.

below: Kim (from the right, fourth person kneeling), among his fellow students at Seoul National University, Korea's most premier school, in the immediate post-Korean War period.

left: Kim (middle, rear) was the leader of the Korean students against Japanese bullies in a middle school in Japanese-Occupied Korea.

above: Kim (left, top), with the students against Japanese bullies. The astronomical tower pictured is in the ancient capital of the Shilla dynasty.

inset: Kim (front row, left), as a young student enlisted in a special unit aiming messages to North Korean troops during the Korean War.

above: Kim and his second son, Hunchul, honor Kim's mother, who died during the Korean War, at the gravesite, in the Korean Confucian tradition.

left: The young National Assemblyman Kim, his wife, with two of their eventual five children.

above: With his wife, on the occasion of Kim's 60th birthday.

right: Kim with Pope John Paul II in one of his many meetings with world leaders.

below: Kim uses the good offices of President Mikhail Gorbachev to talk with North Korean representatives in Moscow in 1990.

left: The young politician Kim visits Japan, home of Korea's former colonial "masters."

above: Former U.S. Secretary of State Henry Kissinger told Kim he should move into a fancier house.

above: Kim in one of his several encounters with President George Bush.

right: Lt. Gen. Ronald R. Fogleman, Commander U.S. Seventh Air Force, talks to Kim about new electronic weaponry.

left: Kim's mountain-climbing club was a fellowship organization. He and the members participated in long walks to discuss democracy and its meaning for their country.

below: At the Demilitarized Zone looking over the border into North Korea with a view toward unification.

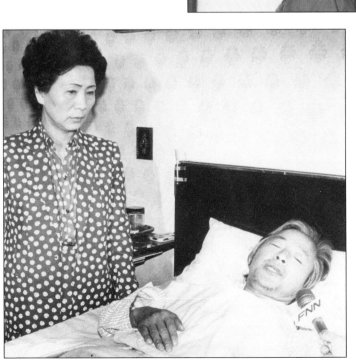

left: Kim staged a 23-day hunger strike in 1983, one of many attempts to bring democracy to Korea.

top: Honoring a student martyr killed while undergoing police interrogation.

above: The new allies: President Roh Tae-woo, who ran against Kim, and whose government party merged with Kim Young-sam's opposition to form a new, broad, middle-of-the-road majority.

top: Kim (third from right) participates in annual planting of rice. Rice farming remains a ticklish political problem. More than 60 percent of Korean farmer income comes from rice crops.

left: Waving the banner of the new united Democratic Liberal Party of Kim, Roh, and Kim Chong-pil. Kim is now the official candidate of the Presidency.

above: Carted away by the police after participating in a demonstration, one of many such episodes in Kim's 30 years in the democratic opposition.

top: Meeting Mrs. Sakharov.

above: The Kim family with Kim's 82-year-old father, owner of the family dried-fish business.

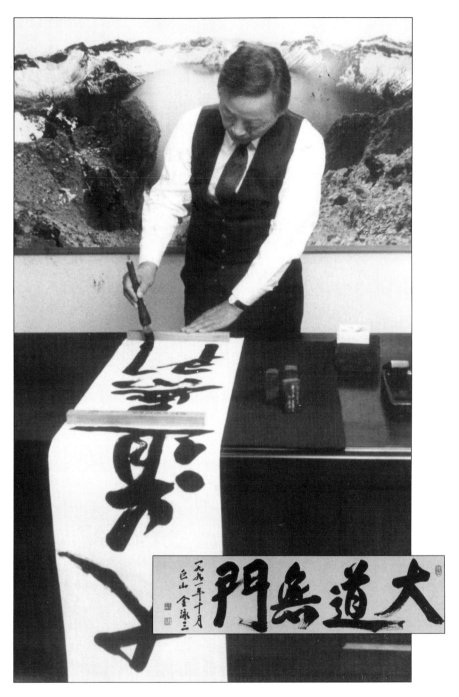

above: Executing the ideographs of Chinese calligraphy. As a high school student, Kim Young-sam wrote the symbols, "Future President of Korea: Kim Young-sam" in Chinese calligraphy.

inset: Kim's completed calligraphy.

six

The American connection

"In the late 19th century and before World War I, American leaders did not intervene when our independence was snuffed out by the Japanese," Kim Young-sam says. "In fairness, of course, it must be said that Korea did not figure much then in the U.S. view of the world. Nor did American power play the role it has since World War II in deciding the issues of international affairs.

"But you Americans, as we Koreans, of course, were to pay for that negligence. It was the beginning of a long series of events brought on by Japanese imperialism and militarism that culminated in Pearl Harbor. It was to cost us, the Koreans, 50 years of brutal Japanese occupation, and to cost you Americans, thousands of lives and enormous resources in World War II.

"Again at Yalta, Cairo, and Potsdam, when the leaders of the anti-Nazi alliance and anti-Japanese coalition met, the problem of Korean independence and integrity fell between the cracks. In the Korean War, which came about because of that indecision and the division of our country after the Japanese surrender, both the Korean and American peoples paid a heavy price for those lapses and mistakes in policy.

"But having said all that, I want to make it crystal clear that I believe—and I believe it is the view of the great majority of my compatriots—that we Koreans owe the American people an enormous debt," Kim continues. "Had it not been for the self-sacrifice of young American men here in that dreadful war, had it not been for American generosity and kindness which followed the war, the peace and prosperity that you see about you in our country today would never have been possible," Kim says with great fervor.

"Furthermore, we owe the Americans another debt: To our own rich heritage of culture and art, America has been our window on the Western world. Your idealism has always been an inspiration to us. Many of your missionaries, educators, and doctors came here and devoted their lives to raising the aspirations and strengthening the confidence of all of us in Korea. Especially during the Japanese colonial period, that tiny handful of American idealists were an inspiration to my family and other Korean families like mine. They helped us hold up the torch of Korean culture and self-respect and self-esteem for our own identity when everything was being done to discredit it. It is a part of our history that our young people—so quick to criticize as young people are—do not appreciate.

"I, personally, in the long years of fighting our own authoritarian system, could always look to some of these individual Americans and to your own heroes for inspiration and help. For all this and from the bottom of my heart, I wish to thank you!," Kim says with some passion.

"And one way of doing that, of expressing our gratitude in a practical manner, is to set up new cultural and scientific exchanges; we need to educate our young people about American values which, I believe, are also an important part of why your technological standards are the world's highest. From a purely practical standpoint, we need to learn those principles from you. Without them, we shall never have indigenous scientific development as well as maturing democractic institutions."

Kim Young-sam voices a general and genuine feeling among Koreans. Of course, Americans will not find Koreans universally uncritical of U.S. action, nor will Americans find them glossing over differences with Washington policy and American culture (as could happen in other Asian nations where traditional etiquette requires that all confrontation be avoided). But there is in South Korea in 1992 a profound and abiding admiration and warmth toward and a feeling of solidarity with Americans that transcends politics and the occasional outburst of student agitation and even violence against American installations here.

It is to the American model of individual freedom and democratic principles that Kim Young-sam and the Korean opposition appealed during the long years of strife and authoritarian rule in the South.

The ideological, economic, and structural collapse of the Communist societies has enhanced the appeal of "the American model" (with all its warts) among Koreans all that much more. This is true even among those Korean intellectuals who had been among its greatest critics since the end of World War II. Furthermore, the great majority of South Koreans—headed by Kim Young-sam—believe that the American role on the ground in the Republic of Korea is not ended.

"So long as the North Korean army is as strong as it is and deployed as it is in an aggressive stance on the DMZ, we need American troops here to give us strength, particularly in the form of the newest hi-tech weapons.

"And, lastly, we Koreans are just emerging into the light of a democratic system. To a considerable extent, whether it works or not will depend on public confidence. And whether Americans are comforted by the idea or not, our people see your presence here as a confidence-building and stabilizing factor."

The legal basis of the U.S.-South Korean alliance is the Mutual Defense Treaty of 1953, which morally commits both nations to come to the other's defense in case of attack, although it does not—as in NATO—require an automatic response by the U.S. President. Under the treaty, a Republic of Korea/United States Combined Forces Command with an American four-star general at its head, directs the joint armed forces it established. In the summer of 1992; there were some 36,000 soldiers, 8,000 other U.S. Department of Defense employees, 12,000 Air Force personnel, 500 Marines, and 20,000 U.S. dependents in South Korea scattered over 120 military installations, residing in almost 2,000 housing units. It was estimated by American sources that the U.S. Forces in Korea contributed more than a billion dollars to the Korean economy in fiscal year 1987 through various expenditures and private purchases.

On the other hand, Korea picks up a significant part of the tab for U.S. forces stationed in the country. In July 1992, the Koreans agreed to pay $220 million toward the local currency costs of the American forces stationed in Korea in 1993. That was calculated to be about one third of the total *won* costs. (The total outlay for American forces in Korea is a more ambiguous figure; for example, salaries and many other costs would not be reduced were the forces to be stationed in the U.S. or some other part of the world.) The Republic of Korea is scheduled to pay an increasing portion of these costs over the next few years, assuming one hundred percent of all *won* costs by 1995.

The legal situation of U.S. forces in Korea is further complicated since the American commander also remains the commander of United Nations forces committed in the original defense against North Korean aggression in 1950. The U.S. command presides over the longest truce in the history of modern warfare—beginning on July 27, 1953, after long and tortuous negotiations over two years to end the war. No final peace agreement has been drawn although *pro forma* meetings continue at Panmunjon in the Demilitarized Zone between the two Koreas with the United Nations/U.S. Command represented.

The joint command places South Koreans and Americans alternately in chief and deputy positions. Historically, joint annual exercises of the combined forces—called Team Spirit—have been held, with the exception of the past two years. Seoul and Washington have felt that these exercises have been necessary to maintain military readiness. For North Korea, they have become a ritualistic object of protests and sometimes minor action. In fact, North Korea and China are notified in advance of the exercises and have a standing invitation to send observers. In 1990, Polish officers (Communist Poland was originally a member of the armistice supervision team) sent observers for the first time and confirmed that the exercises were defensive in nature.

Just as the participation of a Polish non-Communist representative is obviously a result of the cataclysmic changes taking place on the world scene, the order of the long frozen negotiations may be changing. During the 1989 Team Spirit exercise, sports representatives from North and South Korea met twice to discuss arrangements for a joint Korean team at the 1990 Asian Games. In 1991 and 1992, because of the high level contacts then taking place between North and South, the Republic of Korea canceled the exercises as a symbol of their willingness to meet the North Koreans halfway.

Yet there is a long record throughout the armistice of continued violations by Pyongyang of the letter and spirit of the truce—through sea infiltration along the coastlines of specially trained teams, through violence at the Panmunjon meeting place, or more recently, through a bizarre series of tunnels discovered to have been built under the Demilitarized Zone intended, apparently, to permit rapid deployment of *spaetnatz*-type demolition and terrorist squads and mobile equipment behind South Korean lines in the event of an attack on the South. In 1974, a North Korean sympathizer from Japan, in an attempt on the life of President Park Chung-hee at a public gathering, shot and killed Mrs. Park. In 1983, 13 ranking Korean officials, including the deputy prime minister and three cabinet members, died as a result of a bombing by North Korean terrorists during a state visit to Rangoon. In 1976, two American army officers were brutally hacked to death in an unprovoked attack by 30 axe-wielding North Korean Communist security guards in the joint security area of the truce conference installation at Panmunjon. In 1984, Seoul security agencies learned that the South Korean film actress Choi Eun-hee and director Shin Sang-ok, missing from a visit to Hong Kong since 1978, had been kidnapped to North Korea. In 1987, a South Korean airliner was blown up over the Burma air space with a bomb planted by a North Korean agent.

The list goes on and on. North Korean state terrorism has been a permanent feature of the regime, often working with other state terrorist groups in places as far afield as Mexico in 1960 and, with the Sandinistas, in Nicaragua in the 1980s. Thus, if American policy was conditioned to treat the issue of the two Koreas and the division of the peninsula as a part of the worldwide conflict between the superpowers, the Pyongyang regime had given ample justification for such a view.

This U.S.-on-the ground commitment to the defense of South Korea has been questioned only once since the end of the Korean War, and that was by candidate (and later President) Jimmy Carter in 1975. During the campaign Carter told *The Washington Post* that he saw no reason for American troops to be stationed in South Korea and that, if elected, he would pull them out along with the nuclear weapons stationed there. Carter apparently wanted to remove the "trip-wire" U.S. force to avoid any possibility of an American entanglement in a future land war in Asia. But Carter also appeared to be motivated by his and his advisers' deep antagonism to the authoritarian government in South Korea and its violations of human rights. It appears that they were also heavily influenced by the so-called Koreagate scandal of 1971 involving a lobbyist for South Korea, Tong-sun Park, with ties to the Korean Central Intelligence Agency.

While some of Carter's foreign policy advisers argued that the U.S. troops were not needed for the fundamental stability of the peninsula, the joint chiefs of staff warned of the superiority of the North Korean forces. Although the joint chiefs recommended a scaling down of the American forces, they still cautioned that North Korea might try to use its larger military contingent to unite the country. Their argument was enhanced in early 1977 when the third in a series of tunnels secretly dug under the Demilitarized Zone was discovered. The U.S. Senate in a 77-to-15 vote refused to endorse Carter's withdrawal scheme and the House of Representatives Armed Forces Committee drew up legislation to block the plan. It argued that, in addition to the strategic questions such a move would raise, keeping an American soldier in Korea did not cost more than maintaining that same person in the United States.

Furthermore, critics of the Carter initiative argued that decreasing American power in the area would make U.S. demands on the Park Chung-hee regime for human rights reforms less effective. These individuals drew the opposite conclusion from those advocates of U.S. troop withdrawals who justified their position partly because of the South Korean human rights record. In February 1979, Carter, on the basis of a reappraisal, said no further withdrawals would take place until the end of his administration. A new strategic evaluation of North Korea's strength was the face-saving device which permitted the reversal of policy.

"Yet the United States was unable to disassociate its military commitment to South Korea from its politico-ideological one," Nam Joo-hong writes. "As the reversal of Carter's troop withdrawal policy indicated, the consequence of any major changes in current U.S. commitment to this strategically sensitive area was thought too uncertain yet to risk. Having been militarily committed to the defense of South Korea for three decades, the United States found it inherently difficult to identify some political commitment from which some military involvement was not sought."[13] Nam wrote those words at the beginning of the Gorbachev era, before the dissolution of the Soviet Union, and before some of the cataclysmic events in Eurasia which have followed it. But the arguments, in their general intent, still apply.

In April 1990, the East Asia Strategy Initiative report to the Congress by the U.S. Department of Defense outlined a strategic framework for the Pacific Rim for the 1990s and beyond. The report was a response to a call from the Congress initiated by Senators Sam Nunn (D., Ga.) and John Warner (R., Va.) the previous year, asking the Department of Defense to define its policies more succinctly in the region. The report recommended restructuring U.S. force levels in the region to enable the United States to maintain an effective long-term deterrent relationship with the armed forces of the Republic of Korea. It is envisaged that Korea would take on the leading role in providing for its own defense, while U.S. forces make the transition to a supporting posture. The Defense Department paper reflects a number of new considerations in the U.S.-Korean alliance including American force modernization, a revised assessment of North Korean strength, the enhanced capabilities of the armed forces of the Republic of Korea, and, of course, growing U.S. budgetary considerations.

However, the discovery of the possibility that North Korean scientists were working secretly on a nuclear weapon has increased tension, and all "drawdowns"—force reductions—of U.S. forces in the area have been put on hold. The traditional command patterns on the peninsula have been modified. The modifications acknowledge the changing world scene as well as the growing abilities of the South Korean military: A Korean general has been appointed the United Nations Command Representative to the Military Armistice Commission, and a second Korean general has been named to command the combined ground forces in Korea. Seoul is committed to sharing an increasing proportion of the total cost of the combined military establishment. The Nunn-Warner Initiative originally recommended a three-phase transition to a new situation, with the first phase already begun. It foresaw a streamlining of U.S. forces through a 7,000-head reduction by the end of 1992. Further adjustments were to be made in phases two and three depending on a reexamination of the situation on the peninsula.

Kim Young-sam, representing a very broad consensus among South Korean leadership circles, still believes that the South Korea-U.S. alliance is the centerpiece of South Korean foreign policy and international relations. "We have a special relationship different from those between other nations," Foreign Minister Lee Sang-ock told an audience in Seoul early in 1992. "The fact that there have been seven summit meetings between the two countries since the time of President Roh's inauguration to President Bush's visit to Seoul early this year bears eloquent testimony to this very close partnership."

Repeatedly since the Korean War, American presidents and secretaries of state have reiterated the U.S. commitment to South Korea's independence. In January 1991, Assistant Secretary of State for East Asia Richard H. Solomon said it again: "We have no higher priority than maintaining our commitment to the security and well-being of the Republic of Korea. A central goal of our policy is to forge a new, more equal security and economic partnership with South Korea that reflects its dynamism and the requirements of a new era . . . For the long term, we look to reunification of the peninsula—on terms acceptable to all Koreans. In short, we seek a secure and developing Korean peninsula that is an integral part of an emerging international system and a dynamic force in the Pacific. The challenge ahead for U.S.-Republic of Korea relations is that of transforming what has been primarily a military alliance into a more equal political, defense, and economic partnership," Solomon concluded.

Kim Young-sam for his part believes that there can be important modifications in the partnership. "South Korea will do what it can," he says, "to help meet the costs of the American military establishment in South Korea and the worldwide demands on the United States as the leader of the democratic nations and the only superpower." Kim says that Korea will do that, not simply out of any sentimental feelings of gratitude for what the Americans have done for Koreans—although that is there—but because "the United States is the only power and the necessary force to be the balance wheel in East Asia, to prevent any ambitions of one of the regional powers to hegemony in the area. No one else can do that job."

In the almost 40 years since the end of the Korean War, relations between Seoul and Washington have stumbled more often than not over the issue of human rights in South Korea. The Carter Administration took a particularly aggressive stand in remonstrating to the Park Chung-hee dictatorship over its treatment of the opposition, including imprisonment and house arrest for Kim Young-sam. Nevertheless, some Korean intellectuals, radicals, students, and members of the opposition have seen the U.S. and its armed forces stationed in Korea as allies of

Korea's authoritarian governments over the last 30 years. American installations have been a particular target for student agitation, some of it violent. In the United States, a subliminal memory of student violence directed against the United States is contrasted with a propensity by Americans to see their country as a champion of Korean freedom during the Korean War and afterward. These conflicting images have been an important irritant in relations between the two countries. U.S. embassy installations in Seoul, Pusan, Taegu, and Kwangju have been targets. In 1989, the ambassador's residence was attacked and vandalized. In May 1990, the U.S. Information Service's Seoul offices were attacked with firebombs. In 1992, getting in and out of the U.S.I.S. library requires such elaborate security clearances that the whole purpose of the installation may be lost. These and other attacks have resulted in serious property damage and the death of a student who was using the Pusan American Cultural Center's facilities when it was firebombed in 1982.

With student agitation and violence only a brief encounter in the 1960s and a rare commodity in U.S. history, most Americans cannot appreciate that student militancy is a long-standing Korean tradition. It was associated originally with the struggle for modernization and the fight against Japanese colonialism. After the Korean War, its focus turned to the autocratic governments in South Korea. It was the Korean student demonstrations in Tokyo in 1919 which started the March First Movement, the first organized effort to throw off Japanese rule. The Tokyo demonstrations were followed by demonstrations in the streets of Seoul which spread throughout the nation, largely among the student population.

Students rose up again in June 20, 1926, upon the death of the last surviving ruler of the Yi Dynasty, King

Kojong, whom the Japanese had usurped. That event brought out an outpouring of nationalist sentiment in the provincial city of Kwangju. Despite intensive efforts by the Japanese authorities to prevent the demonstrations, two student groups were able to mount nationwide campaigns for Korean independence. Sporadic episodes continued with students agitating: for Korean language and history instruction in the schools, against discrimination favoring Japanese students in Korean schools, and for separate schools for Japanese and Koreans. The culmination, the Kwangju Student Movement, exploded in 1929 as the result of an episode involving Japanese students and three Korean female students. A clash occurred between Korean and Japanese students which turned into open street fighting in Kwangju. By early the next year, the Kwangju incident had spread across the country and involved 194 schools and more than 54,000 students. In the end, 582 of them were expelled from their schools, 2,330 placed under indefinite suspension, and 1,642 were arrested.

It was this tradition of student-led resistance to oppression and political activity that brought out the students again in 1960 against the regime of President Syngman Rhee. "In March elections that year Syngman Rhee and his Liberal Party mobilized government employees and the police in particular to carry out the most blatant acts of election rigging. A system experimented with earlier requiring open marking of ballots by voters in groups of three, stuffing of ballot boxes, ballot switching, obstruction of opposition party election campaigning, use of terrorist tactics—the government resorted to all these devices and more."[14]

Student demonstrations against the regime started before the elections in the provincial city of Taegu on February 28 and continued in Masan on the day of the elections, March 15, where they were dispersed by police firing live ammunition. Some hundred participants were killed or wounded. But when the body of a student was found in Masan harbor on April 11, the students took to the streets again, igniting demonstrations in Seoul. At a rally in Seoul on April 18, police agents set upon students of Korea University who were holding a rally in central Seoul. The next day students from all the Seoul colleges and universities demonstrated demanding new elections, the resignation of the Rhee government, and the installation of a democracy. Police again fired on the students, setting off rioting that resulted in widespread arson and violence.

The government declared martial law. When professors of the universities demonstrated in defiance of that decree on April 25, they were joined by students and the general citizenry. Rhee—under pressure from the U.S. government and some of his own advisers—resigned and left the country. The students participated in the restoration of order and the installation of an interim government. The noted Korean historian Lee, writing of these events with some emotion, describes both the students' legendary militancy and political acumen. Both are now a part of Korean political tradition: "The April (1960) Revolution [ed. note, most often referred to as The Students' Revolution] was the first in the history of Korea wherein people armed with nothing but bare fists succeeded in overthrowing an oppressive government. The leading role in this revolution was performed by students. Their loss of faith in the established generation and its political order led them to take their position in the vanguard of the April 1960 revolutionary struggle..."[15]

It is this tradition of student activism that still motivates each succeeding generation of the Korean student population and always makes it kindling for political agitation. Although there have been recent instances, as late as 1989 and 1990; the phenomenon may be dying slowly if not disappearing. This would follow the pattern of student activism in Japan where it championed some of the same social causes in the post-U.S. Occupation era, if not expressing the same political orientation. The collapse of the Communist regimes in Eastern and Central Europe coupled with an increasing awareness by young Koreans of the true nature of the North Korean regime may be moderating student opinion and the views of their leftwing intellectual patrons as well. The Korean government is considering an educational reform which will restructure the university system, and this has also had an effect. The greatest impact, however, has come from the movement toward more democratic forms which has taken place since 1987 under the administration of President Roh Tae-Woo, despite his military background. The students see the prospect of the Republic of Korea's December 1992 elections empowering Korea's first civilian president in thirty years. That expectation may in itself bring an end to the street violence.

Other elements are also in the picture for The New Korea: At the end of 1991, there were more than 30,000 Korean students studying in the United States. The Republic of Korea's government is now heavily larded with English-speaking members who have either studied in the U.S. or spent long periods there working with their American counterparts. In addition, there are more than 1.5 million Korean Americans living in the United States. They have become a part of the U.S. ethnic mix noted for its aggressive entrepreneurial abilities and rapid assimilation, unlike some other emigrant groups. During the 1992 riots in Los Angeles, there was considerable discussion about the Korean Americans who lost their property as riot victims and of purported animosity between the Korean American community and both African-Americans and Mexican-Americans in the ghetto where Korean American businesses were located. There is no doubt that to some extent this concern was justified. But an important point was lost in the discussion: No other recent immigrant group was enterprising enough and had enough self-confidence to establish businesses in poorer neighborhoods that many other American business people would have shunned. This same phenomenon is true in other big cities including New York. The community self-help, the dedication to education, and the commitment to improve the living standards of the family that characterize the Korean-American community have been a model for Americans generally. All these factors are bound to have a bearing on the growing commercial and social ties between the U.S. and the Republic of Korea.

As to student violence and anti-Americanism, Kim Young-sam says, "Student demonstrations and violence were a product of our fight against Japanese colonialism and racism and against our own former authoritarian system. I know what the students felt; I have felt it myself. And I was there, often, in the streets with them, fighting against powerful forces that we believed were stifling our country. But I am convinced that in The New Korea we will provide adequate opportunities for lawful and full discussion of all issues. A democratic system offers the possibilities through a free press and free speech to ventilate all expressions of dissent and to change public policy when it runs counter to the will of the people.

"Our problem has been that we feared disturbances which would play into the hands of the Communists in the North," Kim says. "That fear was often used in the past to rationalize oppressive and extralegal methods in the South. With the new world situation, with the whole Communist doctrine now totally discredited, and with our own movement in the Republic of Korea toward more democratic institutions; I believe we will no longer have the kinds of violence that have marked our political life for so long.''

If Kim is correct, one of the great psychological impediments to greater Korean-American understanding will be removed. What seems likely now is that Korean-American relations will revolve much more around those economic issues which have emerged over the past few years. That would be only a natural result, perhaps, of the vast expansion of Korean-American commerce. From a mere $150 million in 1960, Korean-U.S. trade has expanded 250-fold. Trade between the two countries in 1991 topped $37 billion, with the U.S. as Korea's most important single market, buying about one-third of all the Republic of Korea's exports for some $20 billion. (In the first half of 1991, the U.S. took 43 percent of all Korean cars exported, 29 percent of its electronics exports, 19 percent of its textiles, and 50 percent of its shoes and leather goods.) Korea is America's seventh largest trading partner, with total trade comprising about 3.5 percent of all U.S. exports and imports. Although Korea ran trade surpluses with the U.S. during most of the 1980s, the deficit turned in America's favor in 1990.

With this vast increase in business, it was inevitable that problems would arise between Washington and Seoul. The Americans have pressured the Koreans for more access to their market. In July 1991, Ambassador Donald Gregg argued that while the Koreans have removed overt tariff barriers; there are secondary barriers to imports that prevent Americans from competing in the market. The U.S. claims that there are administrative and standard controls, informal quotas, licensing procedures, technical and purchase requirements, and special taxes which prevent the entry of U.S. products. Standards of testing for safety, public health, or consumer information are used to keep out American products. Washington argues that such regulations should be adopted in a transparent and nondiscriminatory manner in order to give equal access to U.S. products.

The American argument is that not only do these restrictions punish the American exporter to Korea, but that they keep internal prices high on many products and make the Korean economy less efficient at a time when it must compete even more effectively in the world markets. An example is a U.S. Department of Agriculture study in 1989 that found Korean domestic food prices among the highest in the world, with the average Seoulite spending 73 percent of weekly per capita income on food. (A Bank of Korea study found that, nationwide, Koreans spent 36.7 percent of household expenditures on food. That compares with an average of about 13 percent in Washington, D.C..)

Washington argues that the Republic of Korea can no longer hide behind the excuse that it is a small, Third-World economy. As the Korean diet improves, the need for cheaper relative food prices could be a significant factor in the demand for rising wages, a drive that today may be squeezing Korea out of some markets because of too rapidly increasing costs. Nor, argue the Americans, can Korea's international debt burden be used as the excuse for continued barriers to imports; it has fallen from nearly 50 percent of the gross national product in 1985 to about seven percent in 1990.

Kim Young-sam accepts a good part of this argument.

He is convinced that Korea, for its own good, must liberalize its economy, including imports, and eventually, including food imports. And Kim argues that while that may be burdensome in the short-term, he believes that in the long-run it will benefit the country. Kim also says that agricultural imports must be opened up, but he argues that can only be done over time, perhaps with the kind of deferred schedules that the General Agreement on Tariffs and Trade permits signatory countries, given Korea's still heavy dependence on agriculture. Meanwhile, Korea is already one of the largest importers of U.S. agricultural products, importing $2.7 billion in 1990.

Agriculture in the Republic of Korea—as in other countries—is politically very sensitive. This is true despite the fact that less than 18 percent of the population now remains directly dependent on the land. Most farms are subsistence agricultural plots averaging 1.2 hectares (about three acres) with a total farm population of about eight million people. Kim's plans include an upgrading of Korean agriculture during this interim period to make it internationally competitive, a 10-year program which will require some 42 trillion *won* (about $55 billion). While rice yields in Korea have been higher than in Japan because Korean farmers are using new varieties, herbicides, and additional irrigation; costs are still enormous and must be scaled down through increased efficiencies if the Korean agricultural product is to compete.

Infringement of intellectual property rights is one of the stickiest problems that the U.S. has had with the fast-growing economies of East Asia. This includes the counterfeiting of trademarked products, the unauthorized use of brand names, and the pirating of music- and computer-software. The Korean government has taken steps to protect foreign, particularly American, owners of such products in recent years. The government amended its intellectual property laws such as those covering patents, trademarks, utility models, and copyrights in 1987; and it established the Counterfeiting Complaint Center in the Korea Industrial Property Office. There were 2,053 shops prosecuted for dealing in counterfeit goods at the end of March 1991, nearly a fifty percent reduction from 1988 levels. The annual volume of counterfeit goods was estimated at $58 million at the end of March 1991, a marked decrease from the estimated $124 million in 1988. The government has also submitted to the National Assembly two pieces of legislation which would protect the design layout of integrated semiconductor circuits and an Unfair Competition Bill, also focused on data-processing issues.

Spokespersons for the Korean government have argued that the first of these bills reflects the opinions of the U.S. government and American manufacturers. Without a doubt, the protection of intellectual property is a complex matter and subject to considerable interpretation. The economic impacts are also debated. For example, the Korean government has argued that protection of downstream products may "severely impede general commercial transactions," a claim that U.S. manufacturers reject. The Koreans still maintain that the World Intellectual Property Organization and the European Community do not provide such comprehensive protection as the United States is seeking.

On another front, Korea and the United States are negotiating to establish more liberalized and transparent telecommunications services regulations. Korea has separated network services providers from value-added providers in its reform package. It has agreed to permit foreign ownership of up to one-third in mobile telecommunications and port telecommunications. The foreign investment restrictions on added-service providers, presently limited to 50 percent foreign ownership, will be eliminated by January 1994. The Koreans also claim to have set up clear and transparent regulations in accordance with U.S.-Korean agreements. Additionally, Korea has submitted an application to join the GATT Government Procurement Code and has held several bilateral negotiations with both the U.S. and the E.C. regarding government procurement. The Koreans also say they look forward to joining any new agreements on telecommunications that may come from the Uruguay Round of the General Agreement on Tariffs and Trade negotiations.

In the end, the American-Korean debate on trade is an argument about whether the glass is half full or half empty. "Certain advanced countries may find the level of Korea's liberalization and degree of contribution to the Uruguay Round to be unsatisfactory," says an official publication of the Republic of Korea. "However, considering that the time frame of Korea's rapid expansion in economic scale and trade volume spans only one generation, it is only a matter of course that certain parts of Korea's system, practice, and legislation are still inconsistent with international standards. Moreover, since Korea's success as a small economy is dependent upon freer worldwide trade and a more liberalized regime, the only appropriate policy direction for Korea is consistent pursuit of market opening and liberalization. As such there can be no doubt as to Korea's strong willingness to open its market and to contribute to the multilateral negotiations for free trade."

The American response is found in a question-and-answer booklet on Korean-American relations issued by the U.S. Embassy in Seoul for new arrivals, which states:

"The world no longer regards Korea's as a small economy needing protection; its enormous success as a trading nation belies this misconception. Just as Korea has advanced economically through its partic- ipation in the liberal world trading environment, it now has an obligation to properly preserve and ex- pand that system. . . . Although the Korean govern- ment has published data attempting to demonstrate that market opening moves requested by the United States have mainly resulted in increased imports from Japan, the reasons for this often lie in the man- ner in which Korea has complied. . . . In fact, few of Korea's 'liberalizations' attributed to U.S. requests have resulted in a significant volume of imports from any source, because of the continuance of high tariffs and secondary barriers. The U.S. recognizes that open markets do not guarantee U.S. companies any certain market share. It also realizes that in some cases producers from other countries are more effi- cient and have a comparative advantage over Ameri- can producers. . . . In the United States, Korean companies are also free to trade on the merits of their goods and services. The U.S. government is asking that Korea provide the same fair treatment that the U.S. offers Korea.''

There is some fear in Korea that the new North Amer- ican Free Trade Area (NAFTA) that is being negotiated among the U.S., Canada and Mexico, may negatively im- pact the Asian-Pacific economy, and thus Korea. The Ko- reans do not believe that East Asia has the option of building its own trade bloc if the NAFTA and the Euro- pean Community become more protectionist of their re- spective regional interests. First, they point out that the potential Asian partners have a long history of being sus- picious of each other. Second, the economies of East and South Asia are so heterogenous in their level of sophisti- cation and their interests that it is difficult for them to co- alesce on issues. Third, despite a great deal of rhetoric, little concrete has taken place to align these nations into regional trade alliances.

"It is too early to say what will actually happen," Kim Young-sam says, "but it's not too early to begin to worry. That's why the problems of Korean-American commercial relations are all the more worrisome to some of us. And, of course, there is an additional concern among Koreans when there is any talk of an Asian regional trading bloc: The fact that, simply because of the size of its economy, it would be led by Japan."

"The American-Korean relationship faces the challenges of two relatively healthy economies with strong entrepreneurial foundations in a vast new interchange of goods across the wide Pacific, something even our fathers could not have visualized," Kim Young-sam says. "I cannot believe that our nations will not overcome these relatively minor problems so that our two peoples can prosper in an ever widening exchange of goods and services."

seven

A man's world, a woman's hopes

One of the most often heard cliches of modern life in the Republic of Korea is to assign the blame—and sometimes the credit when something is praiseworthy—for whatever happens in political, social and even economic life to Confucianism. In part, of course, this is a search for a scapegoat. But it is also an attempt to exorcise a powerful ghost, one that dominated Korean life for much of its history.

Confucianism is, of course, a system of morality and ethical conduct in life. It dates back to the ancient Chinese philosopher Mencius. The concept was extremely utilitarian, however, in prescribing a set of precepts for the proper management of society. It saw a human being as an essentially social creature bound to his fellow man through jen, roughly translated as "sympathy". The Confucian scholars said that jen should be expressed in society in terms of five relationships—sovereign and subject, parent and child, elder and younger sibling, husband and wife, and friend and friend.

"Of all creatures between Heaven and Earth, man alone is the most noble, and what is noble in man is that he possesses the Five Relationships"—so goes the first lines of the Tongmong sonsup, The First Exercises of Youth, a Confucian text for properly bringing up a young man. Among the five, the filial bond is usually presented as the most important. These relationships are made to function properly when li, a term combining ritual and etiquette, is rigidly invoked. In most of these associations, some people are superior to and inferior to others. To be treated well by superiors, the maxims hold, one must treat inferiors well—not unlike the so-called Golden Rule of Judaeo-Christian culture.

Virtue in these relationships is not induced through compulsion but by observing suitable models. The ruler of the nation, as the moral exemplar of the whole state, must be above reproach; but Confucianism places a strong obligation on all people to be virtuous. The early Confucian scholars foresaw that the millennium of ethical rule might be in the distant future, but it could be advanced "by the rectification of names." Meaning that examination might be used to deduce to what degree the occupant of a position—for example, an official of an institution—conformed to the highest standards of his role. Thus, a king who charged his subjects exorbitant taxes could be forced through moral suasion to reform. And, lesser officials might be subjected to written examination after long periods of study as a way of qualifying them for positions.

Early, probably before the common era, these ethical principles were combined with more ancient Chinese religious practices and homage was paid to a heavenly deity who ruled over all. He, in turn, could show his displeasure with a ruler on earth by sending natural calamities. Students of Confucius (Kung Fut-se), living from 551 to 479 in the common era and most likely including the disciple Mencius himself, recodified these ancient principles in the "analects"—collections of sayings and dialogues—and made him a figure of worship. Temples were built in his honor, where followers were permitted to make sacrifices and indulge in other veneration to try to divine what was the cause of natural and human disasters. This reverence for the ancient scholar continued down to modern times, although the Communist rule in China has tried to stamp out the Confucian theology (if, perhaps, as some would argue, sometimes adopting elements of its dogma).[16]

This concept of the world and how best to organize it for the good of mankind that was adopted by Korea as the official ideology of the regime when Yi Song-gye, a victorious Korean general, seized power from the Koryo kingdom in the northwestern part of the peninsula at the end of the 14th century. Korea was to be governed under the Yi until the Japanese usurpation in 1910. The regime probably represents the longest and most stable government in modern history. It suffered only two major and devastating interventions from abroad: in 1596 during an abortive Japanese campaign to reach Mongol China and again in 1876 when the marauding power of the Western world began to intervene in East Asia.

Even the turbulent and vibrant society that Korea has

become in the late 20th century still harks back at every turning point to this long history of Confucian thought with its logic and practices. "In the frequent discussions of America in Korean newspapers and magazines, *kaein-juui* (individualism) is commonly criticized as the most serious flaw of Western society. [The] Koreans' greatest fear of their own modernization process is that it will bring rampant *kaeinjuui*.[17] However, some critics see a tendency toward despotism in Confucian culture since the leader rules by providing an example for the ruled, not according to some law (as in the Mosaic code of the West) which is external to and independent of the leadership.[18]

Under the Yi (and the latter part of the Koryo regime), Confucianism mutated to Neo-Confucianism, which put the emphasis on those respects of the older cult which explained the origins of man and the universe in metaphysical terms. Because of this transformation of the original Chinese Confucian concepts, conventional wisdom has it that Korea has a Confucian tradition more deeply implanted than in either China, the place of its birth, or Japan, where it has also contributed heavily to cultural patterns. And critics have said that Neo-Confucianism was an intolerant doctrine, quick to reject all other teachings, because it places undue emphasis on the relationship of the ruler to the ruled, to the exclusion of other relationships in the society.

At the end of the Koryo and the beginning of the Yi Dynasty, Confucian studies of ritual and rules were greatly expanded. In material terms, the National Academy and the National Shrine to Confucius were rebuilt, and ample funds were provided for students of Confucian doctrines. The cultural and literary elite—that special class in Korea and other East Asian societies who devoted themselves to the study of Chinese ideographs—shifted their focus from *belles lettres* to Chinese classics and histories. In fact, a position titled the Superintendent to Teach Classics and Histories was created.

But there was more than philosophical concepts to be gained from the Chinese. Metal movable type was developed in Korea in 1234 for the printing of *Prescribe[d] Ritual Texts of the Past and Present*. Ramie and silk augmented hemp for garments. Cotton was introduced from China in 1363, and a cotton gin and mill were presented to a secretary to a Korean envoy to China. Gunpowder was manufactured under a Superintendent of Gunpowder Weapons in 1377, and cannon were successfully used to fend off the raids of Japanese pirates. In sum, under the Yi, Korea, although isolated from the world except for its contacts with China, was a highly developed society, as one can see. It collapsed, as we have said, in the face of Japanese militarism. Western industrialization and its concommitants came through the Japanese window. But Korea also imploded because its peaceful and stable agrarian society ran out of arable land as the population expanded.[19]

In examining this cultural tradition, historians and economists observed seemingly conflicting conditions: "It is a striking fact that all the areas in which the Confucian ethic has penetrated, have shown, during this century, a remarkable capacity for economic growth, and Korea is no exception. We must conclude that a basic reason for development is that the country is occupied by Koreans. What this means in terms of self-discipline, work attitudes, desire for education and family advancement, and adaptability to change, is in certain respects similar to the values and attitudes brought by Protestantism to the emergence of early capitalism."[20] But in the same book one also finds: "It is tempting to hazard a guess that Korea has developed because it is occupied by Koreans, but this hypothesis hardly explains the relatively stagnant society that existed during the century preceding the opening of the country to external influences."

Yi seized power as the head of a new *literati* class which dominated the bureaucracy. He chose the name Choson for his kingdom, after one of the oldest of the preceding Korean nations, and put the capital at Hangyang, the present site of Seoul (which means "capital" in Korean. The location was to remain the political and cultural center of the peninsula into this century.). The Yi Neo-Confucianist bureaucrats turned their backs on Buddhism, which had been the favored religion in Koryo, and distributed the Buddhist wealth which had been accumulated by the monks in their control of vast temple estates. One of the first actions of the Yi was a land reform in 1390 which redistributed the temple lands. Used as rewards for the Yi retainers and as government lands, these assets established the new regime on a sound financial foundation. Consequently, the Korean peninsula enjoyed universal peace through the next three centuries.

The Yi developed a highly centralized society with no possibility of regional powers challenging the government in Seoul. (It is perhaps that tradition of centralized power—reinforced during the half century of bitter Japanese occupation—which has haunted the Republic of Korea and stimulated the regional dissidence of the post-World War II period.) But the concentration of power in Seoul did not mean concentration of power in the hands of a tyrannical king. By the second half of the Yi dynasty, the king's power was restricted by a mighty bureaucracy which adroitly protected its own power.[21]

Today you will hear Koreans describe various characteristics of Korean society—including their homage to elders, their deep respect for elected officials, their conformity to rituals, and their dedication to education—as part of their Confucian tradition. This is particularly the case in the respectful attitude held toward the educated government officialdom. Certainly the modern Korean bureaucracy has built heavily on it. One may well conclude, for example, that it is this independence (or arrogance) of the Korean bureaucracy which permitted the country to advance at such a rapid rate economically at the very time that political conflicts appeared to be wrenching the country apart. If political stability is assumed to be essential to economic development, one could certainly argue that the Republic of Korea did not have it during much of its recent remarkable expansion.

How was this possible? One answer may lie in the existence of a governing economic bureaucracy which was independent, competent, and far-sighted. It continued to recommend policy decisions and carry them out through all the tempestuous conflicts between a military-dominated government and a civilian-led, politically democratic opposition.

Yet, it could be equally argued that the Confucian tradition has also prevented the Republic of Korea from moving ahead into a period of greater freedom. The mandarin legacy, while it affords an opportunity for an able and self-assured civil service, also impinges on individual freedom. The inflexibility of and the fascination (even obsession) with ritual and formalities often prevents or obscures real communication. At times, this Confucian tradition appears to be in basic conflict with the more emotional, more direct, and more pragmatic aspects of the Korean personality. One has to wonder if the polarization in Confucian thought did not take place in Korea precisely because rituals and rules were laid down more firmly for the more emotional Koreans than for either the Chinese or Japanese.

Nowhere does hidebound Confucian thought rankle more than in the role and treatment of women in Korean society. "Beginning at the inception of the Confucian Yi dynasty, Korean women of the *Yangban* [literary and cultural aristocratic] class lost most of the freedom and independence they had gained under Buddhism," notes Diana Yu, a Korean-American writer. "Watchful censors demanded that *Yangban* women be banned from the streets during the daytime since there was no societal need for them to appear in public. Confucian legislators, 'to rectify the womanly way' and to confine women to the domestic sphere, particularly censured women's frequent visits to Buddhist temples. In 1404, Buddhist temples were declared off limits to women except for memorial services for their parents. Not only were women legally restricted from going to Buddhist temples and shrines, but shamans' [animist priests] houses were also found to have a corrupting influence. Patronizing them was forbidden in 1431. For five hundred years, all through the Yi Dynasty, women continued to be oppressed in every aspect of their lives by Confucianism."[22]

Karl Jaspers, the noted German philosopher, says (according to Diana Yu), "One is struck by Confucius' indifference toward women. He has nothing to say about matrimony, speaks disparagingly of women...and frequently commented that nothing is as hard to handle as a woman. The atmosphere around him is distinctly masculine." "When a hen crows like a rooster, it brings ruin to the home," says an old Korean expression, and states a generally held Confucist sentiment.

Whether, as Ms. Yu argues, the present status of

women in Korea is the result of Confucian tradition, their status in Korea society is certainly less than equal. In 1989, 30 percent of all domestic criminal cases were assaults reported against wives. As in many Asian societies, there is a strong preference for male children. Traditionally women were denied education, and education for females did not come until the Christian missionaries in the 19th century began to establish schools for them. (Today, Korea has the largest educational institution for women in the world, Ehwa University, founded in 1886 by an American female missionary.)

Yet despite this long tradition, women do play a very important role in Korean public life. Three women are members of the National Assembly in 1992. But as in other Asian societies, women are more often important as informal communicators and back-channel power-brokers. Women are expected to play a behind-the-scenes role as intermediaries and intelligence gatherers in business as well as in politics. This is in the tradition of the ki-saeng, women entertainers in restaurants and other nighttime gathering places where the most serious business of politics and commerce is often carried out.

Yet most women in the workplace in 1992 in Korea are not from affluent families. Often, with just high-school educations, they are expected to perform low-paying jobs until they marry and become housewives. By the early 1970s, women comprised about a third of the workforce according to an International Labor Office (ILO) report. Korean women work on the average 54.1-hours per week compared to 50 hours for men. Korean women do have opportunities in professional careers, however—in teaching, in medicine, and, to a lesser extent, in law. With sex discrimination largely eliminated by law, women teachers have had more opportunities. Apparently because Korean folk-healers were women, the acceptance of women practicing medicine is more open; and 14 percent of doctors in Korea are women.

Women have gone a long way toward achieving equality before the law, despite whatever informal discrimination may exist. A new law passed in 1989 forbids sex discrimination in industry; and, although women advocates say that enforcement may not be assured, the very fact that the law is on the books is considered a major victory. The role of women, while a concern behind the scenes in Korean life, is rarely a public issue. A new family law which would amend Korean statutes on marriage, divorce, property rights, the rights of children, and so forth has been debated for some time in the National Assembly.

In addition, the enormous evolution of Korean society in recent years has had other impacts. Urbanization and the changeover from the traditional Oriental extended family system to nuclear families has taken a heavy toll in contemporary Korea. The rapidly lengthening lifespan—according to recent data, more and more Koreans are now living well into their 60s and 70s—has brought the problem of caring for the aged to South Korea much more quickly than expected.

The emphasis on respect for elders is a heritage of the Confucian ethic. But, as more people live longer, Korean government planners foresee many problems erupting. A whole section of industry, they believe, must be created to produce jobs for the elderly. In 1991, the Labor Ministry intended to introduce legislation making it mandatory to offer jobs to elderly people. "But it is obvious that expanding job opportunities for seniors is not a political measure," Kim Young-sam says. The law would affect only such positions as toll collectors, railroad crossing guards, traffic wardens, and parking attendants. Not only are these jobs limited and likely to disappear with increased technological sophistication, but there is also increasing political pressure for a wider selection of job opportunities. "If there is job training for the elderly, they would have more job opportunities, but our current social structure cannot keep the balance of supply and demand," Kim contends. "We need to focus on long-term measures, because the problem is going to get a great deal bigger ten or twenty years from now."

Moreover, South Korea is just beginning to feel the effects of the worldwide drug-addiction epidemic. The incidence of drug-related juvenile delinquency has increased, although it has not reached the proportions of the U.S. or Western Europe. Prevention of drug abuse in Korea as elsewhere is primarily a problem of discovering why young people are attracted to drugs. The Korean educational system—with its enormous competition, the family pressures to achieve, and the use of school examinations to a much greater extent than in the West—produces enormous anxieties and strains among Korean adolescents. The passing of the college entrance examination in Korea, to cite just one example, is a major psychological trauma.

And there is a growing movement to reform the Korean educational system in order to eliminate some of the unnecessary anxiety, especially in the formalities of passing from one tier of schooling to another. According to a recent survey, 90 percent of all high school students have dangerously intense emotions concerning the decision about whether to go to college, which college to choose, and how to pass its entrance examination.

Korea has its own "baby-boomers" as well. Despite the recent rather sharp fall in the birth rate, young people between the ages of 9 and 24 make up 31.7 percent of the population. The 20-to-24-year-old age group accounts for one third of that. (About a third of all voters are young people in their twenties.)

"Unfortunately, our educational system is textbook oriented, mesmerized by examinations and rote learning," Kim says. "I am afraid that is the negative side of our Confucian inheritance." Kim proposes a vast educational reform with these aims:

To put the educational system on the basis of student aptitude rather than formal institutional requirements. Korean students, for example, who apply to a university must now choose a particular major and often pick one of the prestigious schools in Seoul. When rejected for that specific discipline or school, they cannot enter another major or university no matter what their academic standing was in previous schooling. "We need to raise the prestige of schools outside Seoul, which may be as good as those in the capital in many ways but which need additional funds and attention from the educational establishment," Kim insists. "I hope we can make that changeover as early as 1994," he continues, "to put college entrance examinations, generally, on a more rational basis. Today the whole process is so inflexible that tens of thousands of students who fail the examinations find their lives ruined; they are unable to enter other professional training programs and often end up with frustrated lives, or even in crime."

"Our whole educational process is geared to old-fashioned literary standards that do not cope with the modern world," Kim observes. "I appreciate that the humanities are important, even essential, and that they form the core of all human knowledge. But in this new highly competitive world, our economy demands technologists and technicians. We need a whole new track for vocational training both in high school and at the more advanced levels. We need vocational training capped by a major new technological institute. That kind of facility is required to bridge the very real gap that now exists between our theoretical knowledge and a practical application of it. We must train literally millions of new technological workers in the next decade.''

Kim hopes that the general reduction in world tension will eventually be felt on the Korean peninsula, thus freeing funds now spent on defense for additional educational expenditures—particularly for teacher training. He is also encouraging some of Korea's largest corporations to enter the educational industry as entrepeneurs.

The role of Christian missionaries and Christianity in changing the moral atmosphere of Korean society has been considerable. In introducing European and Western concepts of morality and behavior, the missionaries opened new vistas to traditional Korean society. It is a subject of debate as to how deeply these new morés and folkways have affected the average Korean. But it is clear that nowhere in Asia, with the exception of the Philippines, has Christianity penetrated so deeply into the fabric of society than in Korea. That in itself suggests a flexibility that belies the so-called Confucian tradition of inflexibility in the Korean culture.

Catholicism began to reach Korea from China in the 1790s and found converts, despite persecution which intensified after the Jesuits lost their battle to make Chinese ancestor worship acceptable to the Holy See. One of the Yi representatives at the Ming court in Peking was baptized. A second wave of Christianity reached Korea in the mid-1900s with Protestant missionaries. In Korea, as in other places in the Far East, the missionaries arrived aboard warships and merchant ships and the Koreans were well aware of the mixture of religion and politics. The Japanese colonial administration put great pressure on Korean Christians, and it can be argued that to some extent the present "success" of Christianity in Korea can be ascribed to its political character as a form of resistance to the Japanese. Christian students, for example, were prominent in the original March 1 Movement of 1919 for independence. Ironically, the main center of Korean Christianity was in Pyongyang, now the capital of the Communist North; and, in part, this explains why hundreds of thousands of Christians from northern Korea fled south before and during the Korean War. The Communists, of course, have tried to stamp out the practice of Christianity in North Korea.

Today, Christianity is the largest organized religion in Korea. Statistics seem to indicate that at least 20 percent of Koreans are nominal Christians. But the contemporary media put the figure much higher, as much as 50 percent in 1992. In recent years, there has been a phenomenal growth of Christian sects in Korea. One contemporary Korean scholar suggests that Christianity was welcomed by the Koreans because they had no native religion such as shinto in Japan or the mixture of Buddhism, Taoism, and Confucianism in China. And, he intimates that the highly emotional personality of the Koreans was fertile ground for Christianity. That may be evidenced in contemporary Korea where the evangelical and fundamentalist churches seem to be gaining large numbers of converts. Perhaps the greatest contribution of the missionaries—and, again, one of the explanations of the penetration of Christianity—is that traditionally the missionaries have devoted themselves to education and medicine. Many of Korea's finest universities were founded by

Christian missionaries and their atmosphere of liberalism and rationality has fed the Korean drive for education—as well as the appetite, as in China, for radical student politics.

If Kim Young-sam should win the presidency in the 1992 elections, a professed Christian will again lead the nation. Already some Confucianists and Buddhists have appealed to him to limit any practice of Christian ritual in the Blue House, the presidential manor. Kim is not likely to violate any unwritten laws about displaying anything but traditional Korean ritual and practices. But he is aware of the need to employ organized religion as a way to help bridge the gap in moving from more authoritarian forms to pluralistic democracy. Although a Presbyterian, he had a warm and apparently successful audience when he visited with Pope John Paul II in Rome. Both Kim and his wife are practicing Christians and attend their church on a regular basis. Mrs. Kim, away from the cameras and the press, has devoted a great deal of her time to volunteer church-related work for the elderly—especially in visiting homes for the elderly and conducting fund-raising for these institutions. "Korea is not the United States; I will continue to do things in my own way," she said, however, when asked if she, like recent American first ladies, would have a favorite charity or social cause.

eight

The Korea of our dreams

"I believe we are about to move up onto a new plateau of stability, democracy, and prosperity in Korea," envisions Kim Young-sam. "That does not mean, of course, that we will have reached the millennium, nor that we will not have deep and abiding problems, nor that we will not have to continue to strive with our maximum effort to achieve results. But we are within sight of the goals that our grandfathers, our fathers, and our elder brothers have pursued for the past 100 years—a modernized and independent Korea, fully deserving of international respect."

Kim, who is now the leading candidate for president

in the December 1992 elections, has striven for more than
40 years in Korean politics for these goals. He represents
the new, post-World War II Korean generation that has
seen both terrible and excitingly positive things in its
country: He was born and suffered the outrages of the Japanese colonial system, when Korea was treated as a subject nation by Tokyo, when Japanese nationalist militarists
actually tried to stamp out Korean culture, and when millions of his compatriots had to flee to China, Russia, and
even to the hated Japan itself, in order to seek their livelihood.

Kim acknowledges that he was one of those Koreans
who suffered least; he came from a wealthy and secure
home and had the benefits of excellent schooling, fulfill-
ing that prime objective of all Korean families. But at 25,
he launched himself into politics—intent someday on se-
curing the presidency of a Korean republic, although the
whole concept of a democratic presidency seemed almost
ludicrous at the time. Today, he is on the threshold of
achieving his ambition. But he has a sense of vision that
transcends simple pursuit of political office. Kim believes
that the suffering of the Korean people during the past
five decades and his own personal trials and tribulations
as a leader of the opposition to authoritarian governments
have prepared the groundwork for what he calls, ''The
New Korea''.

What would ''The New Korea'' look like?

Kim's program rests on three basic pillars:

1. Korea will become a ''mature democracy'', that
   means a country with a political system granting
   maximum rights to the individual but requiring,

in return, a sense of responsibility from all citizens.

2. Korea will be an economically prosperous nation, and that has to mean one in which disparities of wealth do not preclude an adequate standard of living for all.

3. Korea will once again become a unified nation, through a peaceful coming together of the two existing regimes, North and South, even if that takes place through a phased process of negotiation over time.

First of all, Kim says, the highest priority that any nation must place for its strategies and policies is the creation of a country in which the quality of life for its people is at the highest achievable level. ''That not only means an attempt to give them economic benefits, but it means that they must have a cultural and social life, too, which is at a high level,'' according to Kim. Those demands are sometimes in conflict, he admits, and what is needed more than anything else is balanced growth that works out a logical compromise between what is wanted and what is possible for all sectors of the society.

Kim is the first to acknowledge that past governments of the Republic of Korea—even those he opposed and which forced him into temporary retirement from public life, imprisoned him or put him under house arrest, or even attempted to physically injure him—have nonetheless done a magnificent job of pushing the economy forward. More recently, President Roh Tae-woo and his associates have tried to add a dimension of social welfare as they liberalized the economy and freed the country from political restraints. The fact that in late 1992 the Republic of Korea will hold free elections for its first president from the civilian population in more than 30 years is partial evidence of this success, of course.

But many of the past commitments of the Republic to social welfare and reform have been honored more in name than in fact, Kim says. "Given the long and debilitating colonial period, the postwar chaos, the partition of the country, the incredibly devastating and fratricidal war, it is no wonder that we have not accomplished more on all these fronts. I am, in fact, very proud, as I think every Korean must be, of what we have been able to accomplish in this less than a half century since Korea escaped the twin disasters of colonialism and war.

"But that is not to say, however, that we must not get on with the job," Kim adds.

What is the framework for entering this new era?

Kim believes that the essence of the new era must be stability—a stability which will permit Koreans to take up the more intricate and sophisticated tasks that come with "consolidating the economic experience of the past three decades and fitting it into a new social matrix."

"We must move toward a liberalization of our economy and political system, a decentralization which will not diminish efficiency but which will provide all Koreans with a sense of responsibility for their participation in the whole society. We will also defuse, I am convinced, that terrible regionalist chauvinism which has been the bane of the existence of the Korean people from time immemorial and which has been exacerbated by recent history."

For this to come about, Kim maintains, "We must institutionalize concepts of freedom and guarantees of equality before the law. We must also define our role as a trusted and cooperative player in the growing interrelation among economies and nation states.''

"I cannot, of course, speak of any of these problems without referring to our fellow Koreans in the North," Kim says. "We will continue to extend the hand of friendship to them. And I believe that, forgetting the emotions of the past—while remaining ever vigilant about the possibility of temporary failures and their repercussions—we must move forward step by step. We want to show the people in the North that we are prepared to share some of our new-found prosperity with them through trade and other forms of economic cooperation. I think that can be done on a project-by-project basis, and should be done because it will be mutually profitable.

"In the new world of technological and political change, there may arise many opportunities to find a basis for that step-by-step approach. We have already been able to do that with former enemies—in Japan and on the China mainland. And we plan to be among the first to do so when Vietnam is prepared to accept our approaches."

Kim says that the step-by-step rapprochement with the North will add resources to the Republic of Korea by lowering expenses for military preparedness and funding a program of economic aid and investment in the Northern economy on terms mutually satisfactory to both. "The fact is that the reduction in military costs which would result from national reunification could be diverted to enhancing the welfare of the Korean people both in the North and in the South. We are, of course, fully aware of the difficulties ahead. It is rewarding for us to study the German experience. But in certain ways, I believe that we need not be pessimistic: The two Koreas, perhaps more than the two Germanys, are complementary—we were in the past, and I think we shall be so again. The burden of reunification would be enormous but there are advantages in many areas that would come out of it—not the least that a united Korea of some 70 million people would provide a market and a drive that will propel us into the first rank of nations, economically as well as politically."

In the meantime, Kim contends, the Republic of Korea must get on with its own program of making progress on domestic issues. "Solving these problems in the context of the South will be a contribution to their solution in a united Korea, when it comes, for many of them are the same problems," he says.

On the issue of "economic democratization", Kim says, "I do not see any contradiction here. Concentration of wealth and control in the hands of too few huge companies will not only stifle competition, but it will snuff out the drive of small companies which in the more progressive Western economies are the main source of innovation and economic progress. Nor do I see a conflict between government and the need to move toward a more liberalized economy—whatever our successes in the past in managing our economy through government intervention, we now realize that the Korean economy is too big, too complex, and too complicated to be run by bureaucrats. We must move quickly to adjust to international conditions. To be at the mercy of government regulation, no matter how inspired and dedicated our government planners may be, would put us at a disadvantage vis-a-vis our international competitors."

The role of the government is important, of course, Kim says. "If we are to move to a society dedicated to the welfare of all, the government must act as a mediator between the requirements for social security and the demands of industry for economic development. In a sense, the two aims are so complementary that they reinforce each other: For instance, when industrial companies build childcare centers, it enables mothers to re-enter the labor market—counteracting the shrinking pool of human resources caused by lower birthrates. This contribution to social welfare by the industrial enterprises, then, is a contribution to our social well-being, but at the same time it helps us in the competitive struggle for domestic and world markets for our products," Kim believes.

Kim asserts that Korean industry on this front and others is making these kinds of socially conscious innovations. Government's role is to facilitate these changes and even to offer tax and other incentives to encourage their more rapid implementation. "We will all have differences in point of view about what is the best way to make progress in Korea," Kim says. "That is inevitable. It is not only inevitable but it is important that we do have different approaches and ideas about what to do about our problems. To insist on rigid, unbending ideological approaches to our problems would be a certain way to stagnate. One of the few lessons of history is that although our ancestors took Confucianism and made it our primary doctrine for 500 years, they turned it into an unbending orthodoxy which was so rigid that it could not change with the external conditions of the world, and Korea fell into stagnation. Now again, in the 20th century, we have seen a rigid orthodoxy called Communism freeze societies and finally degrade them to the point of collapse. Seldom has the world had such evidence that unbending ideology, rigidity, and formula-thinking do not work.

"Highly centralized regimes have failed all through the Eurasian continent because they did not reflect the attitudes of their people and could not, when tested, call on their people for cooperation and sacrifice," Kim observes. "We have a demonstration of that on our own Korean peninsula. What we must construct in The New Korea is a decentralization of power and authority, something that we have never had. We must make local councils repositories of the people's sovereignty. Who knows better what are the interests of our people than those who live among them? We revived those local councils in elections last year after 30 years in disuse. Getting power down to the lowest level of our government will be a central theme of my administration."

While Kim believes local input and participation have crucial importance, he is equally dedicated to overcoming the divisive regional rivalries which have characterized much of Korea's history. As Kim explains, "I want to go down in Korean history as the president who in modern times did most to eradicate the menace of regionalism from our national life. I believe that since I come from the area of the country with the highest population density, I am not the one to tell my own people first that regional chauvinism must go. Koreans must be judged for their competence and their abilities, not based on the region from which they come." That will be done in The New Korea, Kim maintains, by using government economic policy to try to achieve more equitable development.

"Obviously, Seoul has become too big, too gigantic to be managed properly," he says. "I want to begin to look at what we can do to decentralize government administration and other activities away from the capital and to move them elsewhere in the country. This could help relieve the overcrowding and the impossible working conditions in the capital.

"Again," Kim says, "much of this depends on our reaching a working arrangement with our counterparts in the North concerning our eventual reunification. Greater trade between the two Koreas would be an important step. Another would be joint participation in overseas development, perhaps coupling their manpower with our technologically advanced machinery. Such programs can help build a basis for further cooperation and eventual unification.''

Kim believes it may be possible to move some labor-intensive industry to the North, even before reunification. This could help reduce the costs of exports from the Republic of Korea to world markets. Meanwhile, South Korean companies in third countries around the world can start buying raw materials, for example, at competitive costs from the North.

Kim Young-sam says he endorses the possibility of South Korean firms participating in the projected ''free economic zones'' that are now being planned in the North Korea-China-Russia border areas. Indirect routes could be found too, he thinks, for possible direct investment in the North, from Korean entrepreneurs living in Japan or working in southeast Asia.

''The two Koreas must follow Europe in reducing both arms and the possibility of confrontation,'' Kim says. ''I feel certain that we can install the kind of 'confidence building' measures that preceded the more dramatic announcements of arms cutbacks between the superpowers in Europe to the Korean scene.'' Kim shows his understanding that the question of American forces in Korea is a delicate one; but he believes that that question, too, can be negotiated with North Korea through phased, step-by-step agreements. While the method may require a major concession by North Korea, Kim says, it is a question of time and a phased approach.

''Compromise, conciliation and mediation have always been my solutions to political problems,'' Kim says.

"Unfortunately, for 30 years we had regimes which did not see that the democratic process of compromise is the only way a modern society can achieve stability. We are now opening a new chapter in our politics where a give and take, a mediation and compromise, will be the essence of our policy."

In the past, one of the obstacles to any kind of negotiation has been the North Korean insistence that American troop withdrawal was the *sine qua non* of any negotiation. In mid-1992, that Pyongyang position seems to have shifted. But whether it has or not, Kim suggests that there may be a possibility of compromise even in that difficult question. Such a compromise might be a phased U.S. withdrawal to match a de-escalation of the North Korean threat to the Republic of Korea, he suggests; and, of course, that would have to include a satisfactory solution of the threat of North Korea developing nuclear weapons.

Kim's approach to the unification is based on three major principles: self-determination, peace, and democracy. This means that the ways and means to unification must be decided by the Koreans themselves in a peaceful and democratic manner. These principles have almost become the conventional wisdom for many Koreans, as they see no other alternative.

Following this line of thought, Kim's practical policy aim focuses on three directions. First of all, Kim places a relatively heavy emphasis on the importance of maximizing South Korea's internal strength for national integration to the North. Here, the political stability and economic strength of the South are regarded as the key to the success of dissuading North Korea's revolutionary strategy. "The unification effort requires, above all, effective mobilization of the national will and resources," Kim says.

Second, Kim Young-sam holds that South Korea would and should help North Korea's efforts to reconstruct its bankrupt economy in such a way as to induce North Korean versions of *perestroika* and *glasnost*. By doing so, he hopes confidence building measures of various sorts will eventually "open" North Korean society to the outside world.

Finally, his unification policy aims at creating a favorable international environment, conducive to supporting Korean efforts to "Koreanize" the unification issue. It includes creation of a viable strategic cooperation system with Japan, China, and Russia based on the bilateral Republic of Korea-U.S. security relationship.

"That is not a dream," Kim says. "It is simply a matter of what, I hope and believe, my people have learned through all their trials and tribulations of the past century. Just as we have suddenly started to 'take off' economically, I believe we are ready to call together all our intellectual resources and produce our own kind of modern democratic state.

"The most important thing about contemporary Korea," Kim says, "is that it is becoming a pluralistic society. We are not a country of immigrants who bring with them different views, traditions, and lifestyles. I believe that this characteristic gives U.S. society its great strengths. The reality of Korean society is, however, different. We are a close-knit, ethnic people. Our history and geography have made us homogeneous. But we are increasingly a country which borrows from other cultures; and, in the 21st century, we will draw on all our diverse cultural heritages. We want the discipline and structure of our Confucian philosophers who taught us the meaning of discipline, the wisdom of emulating good examples, and the importance of community and community action. But we also want the humanity, the charity, and the empathy of our Buddhist heritage. And, today, we also have absorbed the Christian ethic with its emphasis on the sanctity of the individual and the need for freedom of conscience. Together with modern technology and unity, all these approaches will help us build The New Korea, 'the Korea of our dreams.' "

A selective chronology of Korea in the 20th century

1901

The Yi Dynasty of Choson appoints ministers to a select group of foreign countries for the first time in its history.

1905

Japan forces the Korean court to sign the Korea-Japan Treaty and King Kojong sends his ministers, secretly and unsuccessfully, to ask help from the U.S., Russia, Germany and France.

1907

Emperor Kojong abdicates under Japanese pressure with demonstrations by his people of support.

1909

A Korean patriot, An Jung-gun, assassinates Japanese resident Governor General Hirobumi Ito.

1910

The Japanese take over the police, kill Queen Min, and force the signature of the Korea-Japan Annexation Treaty ending the 500 years of the Yi dynasty.

1919

The former King Kojong dies, setting off national demonstrations, and the independence movement elects a provisional government in Shanghai with Syngman Rhee as prime minister.

1923

Japanese mobs, incited by rumors of a Korean insurrection, lynch ethnic Korean residents in Tokyo after the Great Kanto earthquake; and fires destroy much of the city.

1925

On the occasion of the funeral of former King Sunjong, who dies amid rumors that he has been poisoned by the Japanese, thousands of students demonstrate in Seoul.

1927

Communist groups consolidate.

1929

An independence movement against the Japanese is organized in Kwangju and holds demonstrations.

1931

"The Manchurian Incident" begins Japan's long and ill-fated war for the conquest of China.

1933

Syngman Rhee appears before the League of Nations to condemn Japanese aggression in Korea and Manchuria.

1937

The Nationalist Revolutionary Party convenes an extraordinary meeting in Shanghai and expels leftist elements.

1940

Japanese close down *Chosun Ilbo* and *Dong A Ilbo*, Korean language dailies, not to be reopened until liberation in 1945.

1945

Korea is liberated after the Potsdam Declaration demands unconditional surrender from the Japanese and reaffirms that independence is to be granted Korea. But demonstrations sweep the country later in the year when the Allies, meeting in Moscow, agree on a five-year trusteeship.

The U.S. sets up military government in the South after Soviet troops enter the North a few weeks earlier.

1946

The Communist Party of Korea, in an about face, endorses the trusteeship proposal opposed by nationalist groups, while the Soviets organize the Korean People's Committee with Kim Il-sung as chairman in Pyongyang.

A Korean provisional parliament is organized in Seoul.

1947

The U.S. formally brings the Korean question to the United Nations General Assembly, which endorses the United Nations Temporary Commission on Korea (UNTOK).

1948

The Soviets bar UNTOK's entry to the North.

The Republic of Korea formally replaces the U.S. occupation authorities, followed by the declaration in Pyongyang of the Democratic People's Republic of (North) Korea.

UNTOK observes elections in the South and U.S. forces withdraw.

1949

The Communist Party and its affiliates are outlawed in the Republic of Korea.

The United States recognizes the Republic of Korea's government.

1950

The North Korean Communists launch an attack on South Korea across the 38th parallel and the U.S. goes to the defense of the Republic of Korea backed by United Nations support (in the absence of the boycotting Soviet Union at the United Nations Security Council).

Chinese Communist troops intervene after U.S./U.N. troops approach the Yalu River border with China.

1951

President Truman relieves Gen. MacArthur of his command in a conflict over strategies in Korea, including the possible use of nuclear weapons.

The United Nations allies in Korea accept a proposal for a truce made by the Soviet Union.

1952

President Eisenhower visits the battlefront in Korea pledging to end the war.

Opposition lawmakers including Kim Young-sam are arrested for opposing a constitutional amendment that permits the ruling party to railroad a re-election of President Syngman Rhee.

1953

President Syngman Rhee orders the release of 27,000 Korean and Chinese prisoners of war in an effort to block the truce negotiations.

The Korean Armistice is signed at Panmunjon, and the Korea-U.S. Mutual Defense Treaty is signed.

1956

President Syngman Rhee is reelected president and Chang Myun, the opposition candidate for vice president, is also elected.

1959

President Rhee threatens war against the North without U.S. help. The Japanese government begins repatriation of Korean ethnics living in Japan to North Korea.

1960

President Syngman Rhee is reelected with widespread charges of ballot fraud; the Students' Revolution forces Rhee to resign and leave the country after extensive domestic disturbances.

1961

A military coup led by Maj. Gen. Park Chung-hee takes over the government.

1963

The Park Chung-hee regime founds the Third Republic under a new authoritarian constitution.

1964

Students protest "low-posture" diplomacy with Japan as Park seeks reconciliation with Tokyo.

1965

The Japan-Korea Basic Treaty is signed in Tokyo to reestablish relations between an independent Korea and Japan. The national assembly approves deployment of Korean troops in Vietnam.

1966

The U.S.-Korean status-of-forces agreement covering American troops in the Republic of Korea is signed in Seoul.

1967

President Park Chung-hee is reelected.

1968

A 31-man team from North Korea sent to assassinate President Park is discovered. North Korean guerrillas are captured attempting to infiltrate by sea.

Ground is broken for the Seoul-Pusan expressway.

1969

A constitutional amendment to permit President Park to run for another term is forced through the National Assembly.

1970

President Park announces his willingness to open gradual contacts with North Korea.

1971

Korean ground troops assume responsibility for defense along the entire 156-mile Demilitarized Zone with a partial withdrawal of American forces. President Park declares a national emergency after narrowly defeating Kim Dae-jung for the presidency.

1972

President Park imposes martial law and is elected to a six-year term under a new constitution approved in a national referendum.

1973

President Park proposes that both Koreas enter the United Nations.

1974

President Park issues emergency measures forbidding criticism of the new constitution.

The United Nations Command announces finding tunnels dug by North Korea under the Demilitarized Zone.

President Park narrowly escapes assassination, but Mrs. Park is killed by a Korean Communist-sympathizer from Japan.

1975

President Park imposes an emergency decree forbidding criticism of the Yushin constitution.

1976

U.S. Secretary of State Henry Kissinger proposes a conference of North and South Korea, China, and the U.S. to discuss Korean questions.

1977

President Jimmy Carter announces American combat troops will be withdrawn from Korea in four or five years. The U.S. and Republic of Korea governments announce agreement on Park Tong sun's testimony in an alleged U.S. Congressional influence peddling accusation.

1978

The U.S.-Korean combined command is formed, and the first American withdrawals begin.

President Park is reelected for another six-year term.

1979

A united opposition party is formed with Kim Young-sam as chairman. The National Assembly, under pressure from the Park government, expels Kim Young-sam from its membership, which leads to massive student demonstrations in Pusan and other cities.

President Park and his bodyguard are assassinated by the head of the Korean Central Intelligence Agency.

1980

The interim government proclaims martial law. Students in Kwangju rebel, and there is unrest in other areas.

Gen. Chun Doo-Hwan is inaugurated as president as all four Korean political parties are disbanded.

1981

President Chun Doo-Hwan is reelected by the electoral college as the only candidate.

1982

The government lifts the 31-year-old midnight-to-4 AM curfew.

1983

Japanese Prime Minister Nakasone visits Korea.

A Korean Airlines plane with 269 passengers aboard is shot down by Soviet aircraft enroute from New York to Seoul over Sakhalin Island.

Some 10,000 Korean families are reunited through broadcasts of the Korean Broadcasting Company.

1984

A Korean team visits China for the first time in four decades to participate in a Davis Cup tennis tournament.

1985

President Chun Doo-Hwan frees Kim Young-sam and other political prisoners from a ban on political activity.

For the first time since the division of the country in 1945, people-to-people exchanges take place among relatives and cultural groups between North and South Korea.

1986

President Chun removes the ban on political activity. Kim Young-sam, at a press conference, suggests he is willing to work closely with the North Koreans to promote unity.

1987

Kim Young-sam inaugurates the opposition Reunification Democratic Party and calls for the "civilianization" of politics in the Republic of Korea.

Roh Tae-woo, a former military figure and chairman of the ruling Democratic Justice Party, is officially nominated as the party's candidate for the next presidential election.

Kim Young-sam and Kim Dae-jung fail to agree on a united opposition candidate.

The National Assembly passes a constitutional amendment for direct election of the president, and 26 million voters go to the polls to elect Roh Tae-woo as a minority candidate against a badly divided opposition.

1988

The federation of Korean Industries establishes a consultative body to organize trade with Mainland China.

The U.S. State Department formally names North Korea as a sponsor of state terrorism.

President Roh Tae-woo announces a new plan for reunification. The three opposition leaders, including Kim Young-sam, announce a parliamentary investigation of the Chun Doo-Hwan republic.

The Summer Olympics are held in Seoul without incident after the Republic of Korea refuses to host them jointly with Pyongyang.

President Roh Tae-woo is the first Korean chief of state to address the United Nations General Assembly, and he makes new proposals for a multinational consultation on peace on the Korean peninsula.

North Korea orders television sets from Lucky Gold Star. U.S. Commander in Korea Gen. Louis Memetrey tells a U.S. Congressional hearing that American forces could withdraw from Korea after 1995.

The Republic of Korea and China agree to open trade offices in each other's capitals.

Kim Young-sam meets with the North Korean Council on the peaceful reunification of Korea in Moscow.

The New York Times reports on the possibility that North Korea is developing nuclear weapons.

1989

The U.S. and North Korea establish their first substantive diplomatic contacts.

North Korean coal arrives on a Panamanian ship at Inchon.

The U.S. Information Service facility at Kwangju is repeatedly attacked.

South and North Korea agree to select a joint team for the 1990 Asian games.

The body of a Chosun University student is found in the reservoir at Kwangju.

Kim Young-sam travels to the Soviet Union and sees a North Korean official.

The U.S. conveys a detailed report to the National Assembly committee investigating the 1980 violence in Kwangju.

1990

President Roh announces an agreement to merge the government party and the opposition parties of Kim Young-sam and Kim Chong-pil.

Kim Young-sam meets Soviet President Gorbachev in the Kremlin.

A series of strikes plagues industry.

Japan and North Korea agree to open direct talks.

Korea and China agree to exchange trade offices.

Presidents Roh and Gorbachev issue a "Moscow Declaration" pledging to end the Cold War in Asia.

A fourth North Korean tunnel is discovered in the Demilitarized Zone.

Kim Il-sung meets the Republic of Korea's Prime Minister Kang Young-hoon.

1991

President Roh announces the Republic of Korea will seek separate admission to the United Nations.

Korea announces a $3 billion economic aid package to the Soviet Union.

President Gorbachev meets President Roh on Cheju Island.

North Korea says it has reluctantly applied for separate membership to the United Nations.

The U.N. Security Council votes to accept both Koreas as members of the United Nations.

President Roh tells the U.N. Assembly he is prepared to talk about "nuclear issues" on the Korean peninsula if North Korea abandons its development of nuclear weapons.

President Bush announces a nuclear arms reduction proposal providing for the withdrawal of all U.S. ground-based missiles stationed overseas.

North and South Korean prime ministers meeting in Pyongyang disagree on nuclear issues despite agreement on non-aggression and exchanges.

Sources: Korea Annual 1991, published by Yonhap News Agency Seoul, A Chronology of Events, USIS Korea, Seoul

Appendices

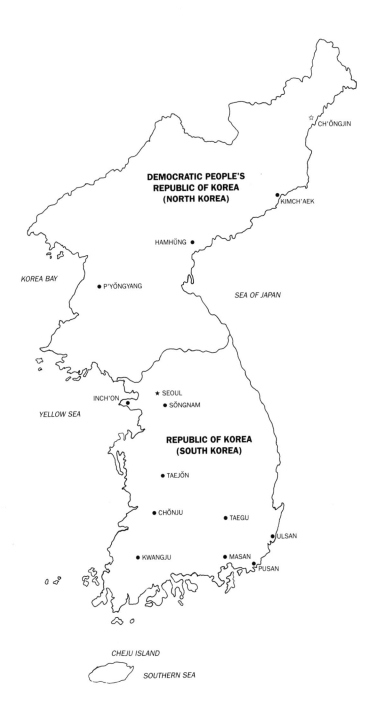

SOUTH KOREA NATIONAL PROFILE

Official name: The Republic of Korea

area: 38,000 square miles (slightly larger than Indiana)

capital: Seoul (population 10.5 million)

other major cities: Pusan, Inchon, Taejon, Kunsan, Cheju, Taegu

government: Republic, presidential

population: 43 million

language: Korean, written in a composite of HAN'GUL, an indigenous script, and Chinese characters

literacy: More than 90 percent

religon: Buddism, Confucianism, Shamanism, Christianity

per capita income: $6,200

currency: Won (approximately 800 to $1, July 1992)

THE NATIONAL FLAG
(T'ae Kuk Ki)

The Korean flag symbolizes much of the thought and philosophy of the orient. The symbol, and sometimes the flag itself, is called T'ae Kuk.

Depicted on the flag is a circle divided equally and locked in perfect balance. The red section represents the *Yang* (plus) and the blue section the *Um* (minus), an ancient symbol of the universe originating in China. These two opposites express the dualism of the cosmos: fire and water, day and night, dark and light, construction and destruction, masculine and feminine, active and passive, heat and cold, plus and minus, and so on.

The central thought in the T'ae Kuk indicates that while there is a constant movement within the sphere of infinity, there is also balance and harmony.

Three bars at each corner also carry the ideas of opposition and balance. The three unbroken bars stand for heaven; the opposite three broken bars represent the earth; the two bars with a broken bar in between symbolize fire; the opposite is the symbol of water.

CENTRAL ADMINISTRATIVE ORGANIZATION

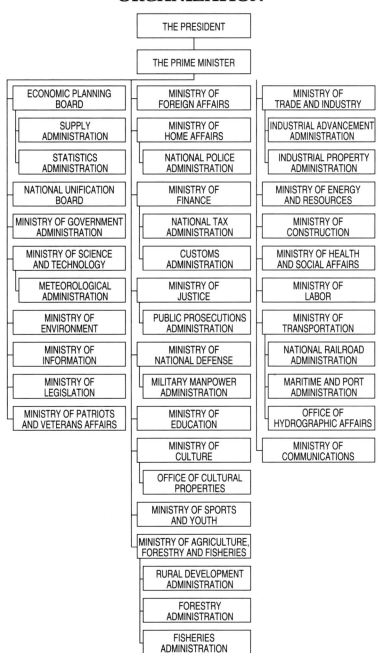

THE PRESIDENT

THE PRIME MINISTER

ECONOMIC PLANNING BOARD

SUPPLY ADMINISTRATION

STATISTICS ADMINISTRATION

NATIONAL UNIFICATION BOARD

MINISTRY OF GOVERNMENT ADMINISTRATION

MINISTRY OF SCIENCE AND TECHNOLOGY

METEOROLOGICAL ADMINISTRATION

MINISTRY OF ENVIRONMENT

MINISTRY OF INFORMATION

MINISTRY OF LEGISLATION

MINISTRY OF PATRIOTS AND VETERANS AFFAIRS

MINISTRY OF FOREIGN AFFAIRS

MINISTRY OF HOME AFFAIRS

NATIONAL POLICE ADMINISTRATION

MINISTRY OF FINANCE

NATIONAL TAX ADMINISTRATION

CUSTOMS ADMINISTRATION

MINISTRY OF JUSTICE

PUBLIC PROSECUTIONS ADMINISTRATION

MINISTRY OF NATIONAL DEFENSE

MILITARY MANPOWER ADMINISTRATION

MINISTRY OF EDUCATION

MINISTRY OF CULTURE

OFFICE OF CULTURAL PROPERTIES

MINISTRY OF SPORTS AND YOUTH

MINISTRY OF AGRICULTURE, FORESTRY AND FISHERIES

RURAL DEVELOPMENT ADMINISTRATION

FORESTRY ADMINISTRATION

FISHERIES ADMINISTRATION

MINISTRY OF TRADE AND INDUSTRY

INDUSTRIAL ADVANCEMENT ADMINISTRATION

INDUSTRIAL PROPERTY ADMINISTRATION

MINISTRY OF ENERGY AND RESOURCES

MINISTRY OF CONSTRUCTION

MINISTRY OF HEALTH AND SOCIAL AFFAIRS

MINISTRY OF LABOR

MINISTRY OF TRANSPORTATION

NATIONAL RAILROAD ADMINISTRATION

MARITIME AND PORT ADMINISTRATION

OFFICE OF HYDROGRAPHIC AFFAIRS

MINISTRY OF COMMUNICATIONS

THE GOVERNMENT ORGANIZATION OF
THE REPUBLIC OF KOREA

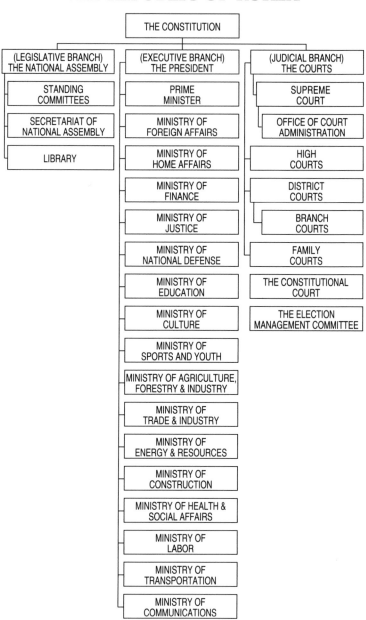

THE CONSTITUTION

(LEGISLATIVE BRANCH)
THE NATIONAL ASSEMBLY

STANDING COMMITTEES

SECRETARIAT OF NATIONAL ASSEMBLY

LIBRARY

(EXECUTIVE BRANCH)
THE PRESIDENT

PRIME MINISTER

MINISTRY OF FOREIGN AFFAIRS

MINISTRY OF HOME AFFAIRS

MINISTRY OF FINANCE

MINISTRY OF JUSTICE

MINISTRY OF NATIONAL DEFENSE

MINISTRY OF EDUCATION

MINISTRY OF CULTURE

MINISTRY OF SPORTS AND YOUTH

MINISTRY OF AGRICULTURE, FORESTRY & INDUSTRY

MINISTRY OF TRADE & INDUSTRY

MINISTRY OF ENERGY & RESOURCES

MINISTRY OF CONSTRUCTION

MINISTRY OF HEALTH & SOCIAL AFFAIRS

MINISTRY OF LABOR

MINISTRY OF TRANSPORTATION

MINISTRY OF COMMUNICATIONS

(JUDICIAL BRANCH)
THE COURTS

SUPREME COURT

OFFICE OF COURT ADMINISTRATION

HIGH COURTS

DISTRICT COURTS

BRANCH COURTS

FAMILY COURTS

THE CONSTITUTIONAL COURT

THE ELECTION MANAGEMENT COMMITTEE

AVERAGE ANNUAL GROWTH RATE OF REAL GNP*

Initial Year \ Terminal Year	1976	1977	1978	1979	1980	1981	1982	1983	1984	1985	1986	1987	1988	1989	1990	1991(p)
1975	13.1	11.4	10.9	10.0	7.1	6.9	6.9	7.6	7.8	7.7	8.2	8.6	8.9	8.7	8.7	8.7
1976	—	9.8	9.8	8.9	5.6	5.7	5.9	6.9	7.2	7.1	7.7	8.2	8.5	8.4	8.4	8.1
1977	—	—	9.8	8.5	4.2	4.7	5.2	6.4	6.8	6.8	7.5	8.0	8.4	8.3	8.3	8.3
1978	—	—	—	7.2	1.6	3.0	4.0	5.7	6.3	6.4	7.2	7.8	8.3	8.1	8.2	8.2
1979	—	—	—	—	-3.7	1.0	3.0	5.3	6.1	6.2	7.2	7.9	8.4	8.2	8.3	8.3
1980	—	—	—	—	—	5.9	6.5	8.5	8.7	8.4	9.1	9.7	10.0	9.6	9.6	9.5
1981	—	—	—	—	—	—	7.2	9.9	9.7	9.0	9.8	10.3	10.6	10.1	10.0	9.8
1982	—	—	—	—	—	—	—	12.6	10.9	9.6	10.4	10.9	11.2	10.5	10.4	10.1
1983	—	—	—	—	—	—	—	—	9.3	8.1	9.7	10.5	10.9	10.2	10.1	9.8
1984	—	—	—	—	—	—	—	—	—	7.0	9.9	10.9	11.3	10.4	10.2	9.9
1985	—	—	—	—	—	—	—	—	—	—	12.9	12.9	12.8	11.2	10.8	10.4
1986	—	—	—	—	—	—	—	—	—	—	—	13.0	12.7	10.7	10.3	9.9
1987	—	—	—	—	—	—	—	—	—	—	—	—	12.4	9.6	9.5	9.2
1988	—	—	—	—	—	—	—	—	—	—	—	—	—	6.8	8.0	8.1
1989	—	—	—	—	—	—	—	—	—	—	—	—	—	—	9.3	8.8
1990	—	—	—	—	—	—	—	—	—	—	—	—	—	—	—	8.4

*At 1985 constant prices.

167

BALANCE OF PAYMENTS IN U.S. $ (MILLIONS)

	1980	1985	1986	1987	1988	1989	1990	1991 (1-10)
Current Account Balance	-5,321	-887	4,617	9,854	14,161	5,057	-2,179	-9,184
Trade Balance	-4,384	-19	4,206	7,659	11,445	4,597	-2,004	-7,774
Exports	17,214	26,442	33,913	46,244	59,648	61,409	63,124	56,070
Imports	21,598	26,461	29,707	38,585	48,203	56,812	65,127	63,845
Invisible Balance	-1,386	-1,446	-628	977	1,267	211	-451	-1,192
Receipts	5,363	6,664	8,052	10,010	11,252	12,642	14,269	12,632
Payments	6,749	8,111	8,679	9,033	9,985	12,318	14,719	13,824
Transfers(Net)	449	578	1,039	1,218	1,448	247	275	-218
Long-Term Capital(Net)	1,857	1,101	-1,982	-5,836	-2,733	-3,363	548	3,882
Basic Balance	-3,464	-213	2,635	4,018	11,428	1,692	-1,632	-5,302
Short-Term Capital(Net)	1,945	-588	-392	-7	1,336	60	3,334	226
Errors & Omissions	-370	-880	-544	1,191	-589	701	-1,976	1,214
Overall Balance	1,890	-1,255	1,699	5,202	12,175	2,454	-274	-3,862
Bank Borrowing(Net)	2,861	1,266	-1,473	-4,009	-1,320	966	1,487	5,055
Foreign Exchange Reserves	6,571	7,749	7,955	9,176	12,378	15,245	14,822	13,580

Source: Bank of Korea

POPULATION GROWTH

	est. (mil.)	annual rate of increase*	density person/km²	North Korea
1973	34.1	1.78	345.3	15
1974	34.7	1.73	351.0	15.45
1975	35.3	1.70	357.1	15.85
1976	35.85	1.61	362.8	16.25
1977	36.4	1.57	368.3	16.7
1978	36.96	1.53	373.6	17.1
1979	37.5	1.53	379.3	17.58
1980	38.1	1.57	385.1	18.03
1981	38.7	1.56	391.1	18.58
1982	39.33	1.49	397.1	18.9
1983	39.9	1.24	402.8	19.2
1984	40.4	0.99	407.7	19.55
1985	40.8	0.93	411.6	19.89
1986	41.18	0.95	415.3	20.24
1987	41.58	0.96	419.0	20.6
1988	41.98	0.97	423.0	20.98
1989	42.38	0.97	426.9	21.37
1990	42.7	0.93	431.8	21.77
1991	43.27	0.92	435.8	
1992	43.66	0.91	439.8	

Source: Republic of Korea, National Statistical Office

* Increase rates are from crude birth rate, crude death rate and emigration rate since 1981.

PER CAPITA
PERSONAL DISPOSABLE INCOME
(in millions of dollars)

YEAR	PER CAPITA PDI	
	Current Market Prices (In 1,000 won)	Current Dollars
1970	83	242
1975	270	558
1976	367	759
1977	463	957
1978	620	1,330
1979	773	1,544
1980	910	1,499
1981	1,110	1,630
1982	1,250	1,708
1983	1,432	1,846
1984	1,599	1,983
1985	1,743	2,002
1986	2,009	2,280
1987	2,326	2,828
1988	2,726	3,731
1989	3,011	4,485
1990	3,549	5,013

Source: The Bank of Korea, (National Accounts)

REPUBLIC OF KOREA
TRADE WITH THE UNITED STATES
1961–1991
(in millions of dollars)

Year	Export	Import
1961	6.8	143.4
1962	12.0	220.3
1963	24.3	284.1
1964	35.6	202.1
1965	61.7	182.3
1966	95.8	253.7
1967	137.4	305.2
1968	237.0	449.0
1969	315.7	530.2
1970	395.2	584.8
1971	531.8	658.8
1972	765.6	648.3
1973	1,021.2	1,201.9
1974	1,492.1	1,700.8
1975	1,536.3	1,881.1
1976	2,492.5	1,962.9
1977	3,118.7	2,447.4
1978	4,058.3	3,043.0
1979	4,373.9	4,602.6
1980	4,606.6	4,890.2
1981	5,660.6	6,049.7
1982	6,243.2	5,955.8
1983	8,245.4	6,274.4
1984	10,478.8	6,875.5
1985	10,754.1	6,489.3
1986	13,880.0	6,544.7
1987	18,310.8	8,758.2
1988	21,404.1	12,756.7
1989	20,639.0	15,910.7
1990	19,360.0	16,942.5
1991	18,559.3	18,894.4

Source: Office of Customs Administration

MIDDLE-CLASS INDICATORS
IN KOREA

Category	1990	1991	1992
Home ownership rate, %	72.1	74.2	75.7
Number of private cars (1,000)	1,902	2,539	3,025
Number of telephones per 100 population	31.0	34.3	37.9
Number of personal computers (1,000)	1,060	1,810	2,710
Average life span for both sexes, years	71.3	71.6	71.9
Male	67.4	67.8	68.2
Female	75.4	75.6	75.9
Population per physician*	886	855	826
Population per hospital bed**	498	470	408
Number of pupils per elementary school class	41.4	40.8	40.2
High school-age children enrolled in high schools, %	86.8	87.6	85.7
High school graduates who enroll in Institutions of higher learning, %***	37.6	38.1	39.8
Investment in science and technology as % of GNP	2.2	2.4	2.6
Households supplied with piped water, %	79	79.5	80.6
Sewage treatment rate, %	31.0	33.0	39.6
Paved road rate, %	71.5	83.0	87.0
Television sets in use (1,000)	7,438	8,344	8,478

NOTE: * Only registered physicians, including Oriental physicians, are taken into account.

   **Only hospital beds for ordinary patients, excluding those for tuberculosis, leprosy, mental and dental cases and those at Oriental medicine hospitals, are taken into account.

   ***Four-year colleges and universities, plus two-year junior colleges.

Endnotes

[1]Alice H. Amsden, *Asia's Next Giant: South Korea and Late Industrialization*, Oxford University Press, New York, 1989.

[2]*The Far Eastern Economic Review*, July 9, 1992.

[3]John Markoff, ''Rethinking the National Chip Policy,'' *The New York Times*, July 14, 1992.

[4]Mark Clifford, *Far Eastern Economic Review*, July 2, 1992.

[5]Nam Joo-hong, *America's Commitment to South Korea: The first decade of the Nixon Doctrine*, Centre for International Studies, London School of Economics and Political Science, Cambridge University Press, Cambridge, 1986.

[6]Nam, *ibid.*

[7]Ki-baik Lee, *A New History of Korea*, translated by Edward W. Wagner with Edward J. Shultz, Harvard-Yenching Institute, Harvard University Press, Cambridge, Mass., 1984.

[8]"Russia looks at the world: Westward ho?" *The Economist*, July 4, 1992, London.

[9]Tong Whan Park, "Issues of Arms Control between the Two Koreas," *Asian Survey*, Vol. XXXII, No. 4, April 1992.

[10]Clayton Jones, "N. Korea's Kim Buttresses Cult," *The Christian Science Monitor*, July 2, 1992.

[11]"Political change in North Korea," *North Korea in Transition*, Eds. Chong-Sik Lee and Se-Hee Yoo, Institute of East Asian Studies, University of California at Berkeley, Berkeley, CA, 1991.

[12]Robert A. Scalapino, *North Korea in Transition*, Eds. Chong-Sik Lee and Se-Hee Yoo, Institute of East Asian Studies, University of California at Berkeley, Berkeley, CA, 1991.

[13]Nam Joo-hong, *America's Commitment to South Korea: The first decade of the Nixon doctrine*, London School of Economics and Political Science Monographs

in International Studies, Cambridge University Press, London, 1986.

[14]Ki-baik Lee, *A New History of Korea*, Harvard-Yenching Institute, Harvard University Press, Cambridge, Mass., 1984.

[15]*Ibid.*

[16]For a description of this vastly complicated and intellectual movement, debated by hundreds of thousands of scholars in the West as well as in the East over the centuries, refer to the *Columbia Encyclopedia, Third Edition,* Columbia University Press, New York, 1963. The basis of the text's somewhat simplistic description is derived therefrom.

[17]Michael X. Kalton, *Korean Ideas and Values*, Philip Johnson Memorial Paper No. 7, Royal Asiatic Society, Korea Branch, Seoul, 1991.

[18]See "Dead Asian Male: Confucius and Multiculturalism," Andre Ryerson, *Policy Review*, The Heritage Foundation, Washington, D.C., Summer 1992.

[19]The first Japanese colonial land survey in 1918 showed the average Korean farmer had only 0.12 hectares, about a third of an acre. Only the Japanese, among major countries at the time, had less acreage per capita.

[20]Edward S. Mason *et al, The Economic and Social Modernization of the Republic of Korea*, Council on East Asian Studies, Harvard University, Harvard University Press, 1980.

[21]The basis for this highly simplified explanation of the Confucianist train of thought in Korean society and

history is Ki-Baik Lee's *A New History of Korea*, Translated by Edward W. Wagner with Edward J. Shultz, Harvard-Yenching Institute, Harvard University Press, Cambridge, 1984.

[22]Diana Yu (Tull), *Winds of Change: Korean Women in America*, The Women's Institute Press, Silver Spring, Md., 1991.

Index

Park Chung-hee, 6, 14,
28-29, 30-34, 41, 64, 98,
100, 103, 151-53
assassination of, 32
Park Tong-sun, 99-100, 154
Park, Tong Whan, 78-79
Patent/copyright protection,
110-11
Pearl Harbor, 93-94
Peking, 129
People's Democratic
Republic of Korea (North),
68-69
Perestroika, 74
Perot, Ross, 89
Philippine Islands, 62
Pohang Iron & Steel
Company (POSCO), 15
Poland, 98
Police raid, 31-32
Pope John Paul II, 131, P:15
Population, 44, 67
baby boomers, 127-28
density, 2
elderly, 126
growth, 43, 169
Potsdam Declaration, 67, 94,
148
Presbyterian, 131, P:12
Prescribe[d] Ritual Texts of
the Past and Present, 121
Price stabilization, 56
Productivity, 45
Prosperity, 135
Prostitutes, 64-65
Protestants, 129-31
Pusan, 26, 32, 71, 104
Pusan American Cultural
Center, 104
Pusan Perimeter, 24-25

Pyongyang, 69, 73-91, 98,
142, 148, 157
Christianity in, 130
regime, 27

Quality of life, 135

Raw material imports, 12
Reagan, Ronald, P:13
Recreational activities
spending, 4
Regional rivalries, 140
Reischauer, Prof. Edwin O.,
31
Republic of Korea (South),
68-69
economic development in,
12-13
Repurchase agreements, 49
Reunification, 6, 27, 31,
73-91, 135, 137-38, 140-44
Reunification Democratic
Party, 35, 156
Revised Foreign Exchange
Management Act of 1991,
50
Revitalizing Reform
constitution, 28
Rhee, Syngman, 13, 25-26,
27, 32, 36, 68, 71, 105-6,
146-47, 150
Rice farming, P:29
Rice pricing, 47
Rice subsidies, 18
Rivalries, regional, 43
Roh Tae-woo, 6-7, 30, 34-36,
40, 75-76, 85, 102, 107,
135, 156-59, P:28, P:30
Rome, 131
Roosevelt, Theodore, 62

The content of this book is based on the input of many interviews and discussions with historians, economists, political figures, governmental scholars, experts on Korean society, academicians in other disciplines, and—most importantly—direct discussions with Mr. Kim Young-sam. After the manuscript was completed, it was edited for style by Ron Beyma.